········· PREFACE ·········

Learning to play a musical instrument is one of the most satisfying experiences a person can have. Being able to play along with other musicians makes that even more rewarding. This collection of Bluegrass songs is designed to make it easy to enjoy the fun of gathering with friends and family to make music together.

The selections in this book include a wide variety of songs drawn from several generations of Bluegrass music. These songs will provide fun opportunities to make music with other players. The music for each song displays the chord diagrams for five instruments: ukulele, baritone ukulele, guitar, mandolin and banjo. The chord diagrams indicate basic, commonly used finger positions. More advanced players can substitute alternate chord formations.

It is easy to find recordings of all these tunes performed by outstanding musicians. Listening can help you understand more about the style as you and your friends play these songs.

Arranged by Mark Phillips

ISBN 978-1-70517-779-2

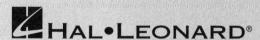

Visit Hal Leonard Online at
www.halleonard.com

World headquarters, contact:
Hal Leonard
7777 West Bluemound Road
Milwaukee, WI 53213
Email: info@halleonard.com

In Europe, contact:
Hal Leonard Europe Limited
1 Red Place
London, W1K 6PL
Email: info@halleonardeurope.com

In Australia, contact:
Hal Leonard Australia Pty. Ltd.
4 Lentara Court
Cheltenham, Victoria, 3192 Australia
Email: info@halleonard.com.au

Standard Ukulele

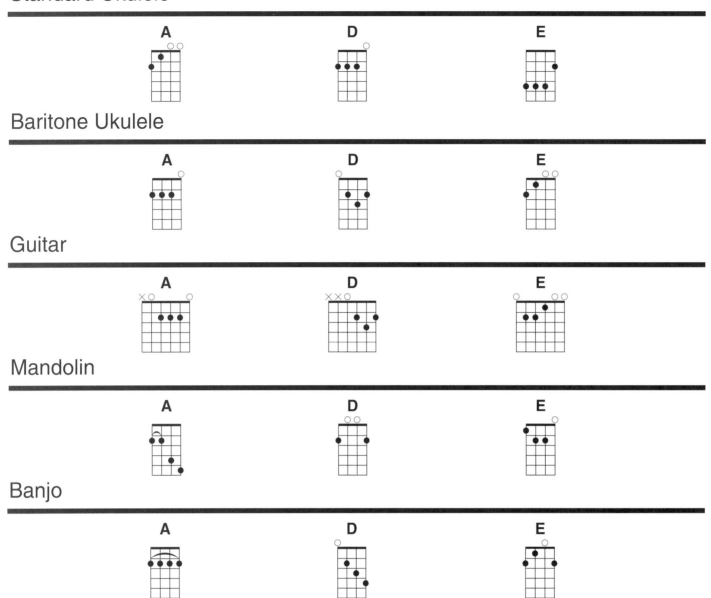

Baritone Ukulele

Guitar

Mandolin

Banjo

Angel Band

Words and Music by Ralph Stanley

My strong - est trials _____ now _____ are past, _____ my tri - umph has be - gun.

whose blood now cleans - es from _____ all sin _____ and gives me vic - to - ry.

Chorus

Oh, come, an - gel _____ band, come and a - round me stand. Oh, bear me a - way on your snow white wings to my im - mor - tal home. _____ Oh, bear me a - way on your snow white wings, to my im - mor - tal home.

1. 2. 2. Oh,

Standard Ukulele

Baritone Ukulele

Guitar

Mandolin

Banjo

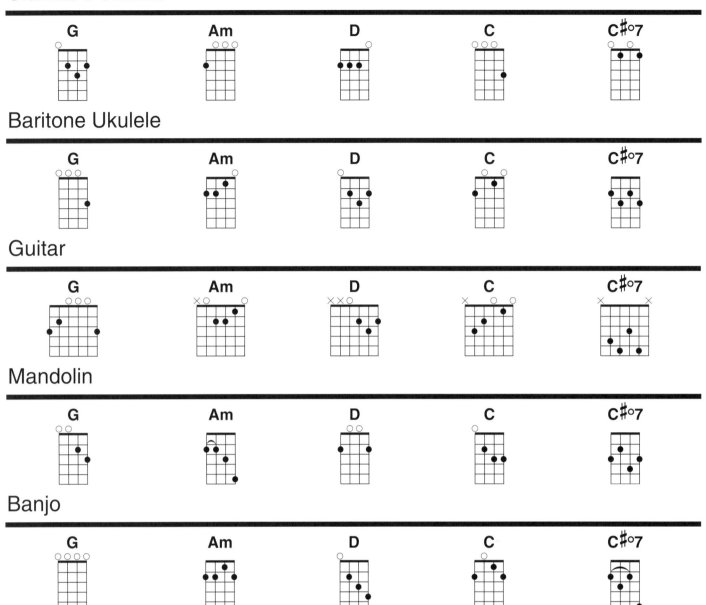

Ballad of Jed Clampett

from the Television Series THE BEVERLY HILLBILLIES
Words and Music by Paul Henning

kept his fam - 'ly fed. And then one
move a - way from there." They said, Cal - i -
kind - ly drop - pin' in. You're all in - vit - ed

day he was shoot - in' at ____ some food, and
for - ni' is the place you ought - a be, so they
back a - gain to this lo - cal - i - ty to

up through the ground come a - bub - bl - in'
load - ed up the truck and they moved to Bev - er -
have a heap - in' help - in' of their hos - pi - tal - i -

To Coda

crude. *Oil,* *that* *is;* ____ *black*
ly. *Hills,* *that* *is;* ____ *swim - min'*
ty.

1.

gold, *Tex - as tea.* 2. Well, the
pools, *mov - ie stars.*

2. *D.S. al Coda*

Coda

Bev - er - ly Hill - bil - ies;

that's what ____ *they call* *'em now.* ____ *Nice folks.* __

____ *Y'all come back,* ____ *y'hear?*

Standard Ukulele

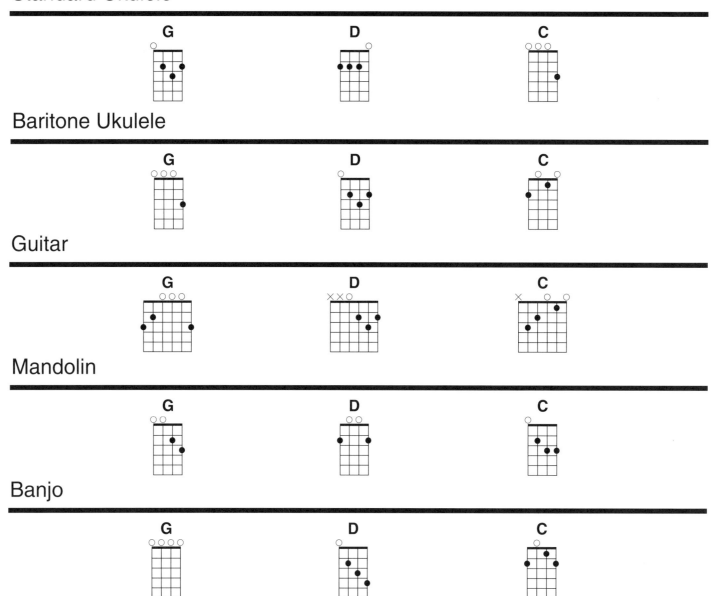

Baritone Ukulele

Guitar

Mandolin

Banjo

Banks of the Ohio
19th Century Western American

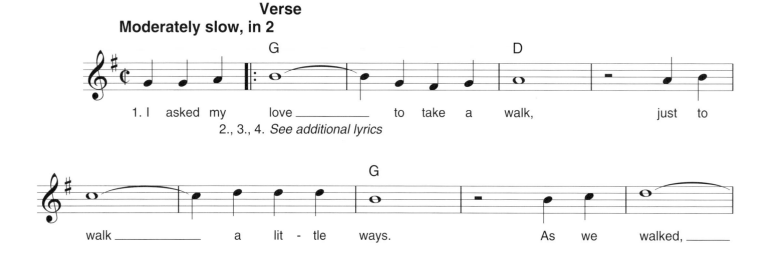

Verse
Moderately slow, in 2

1. I asked my love _____ to take a walk, just to
2., 3., 4. *See additional lyrics*

walk _____ a lit - tle ways. As we walked, _____

oh me, we talked all a - bout our wed - ding

Chorus

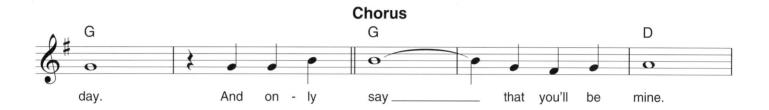

day. And on - ly say that you'll be mine.

In our home we'll hap - py be, down be -

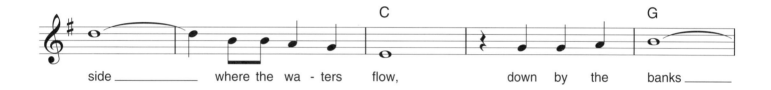

side where the wa - ters flow, down by the banks

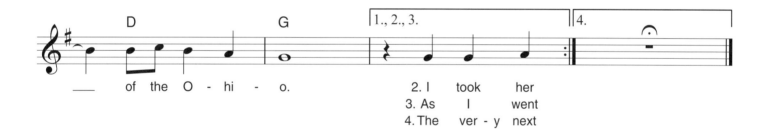

of the O - hi - o. 2. I took her
3. As I went
4. The ver - y next

Additional Lyrics

2. I took her by lily-white hand
   And dragged her down that bank of sand.
   There I pushed her in to drown.
   I watched her as she floated down.

3. As I went home between twelve and one
   Thinking of what I had done,
   I killed the girl I love, you see,
   Because she would not marry me.

4. The very next day about half past four,
   Sheriff Smith knocked at my door,
   Said, "Young man, come along and go
   Down to the banks of the Ohio."

Standard Ukulele

Baritone Ukulele

Guitar

Mandolin

Banjo

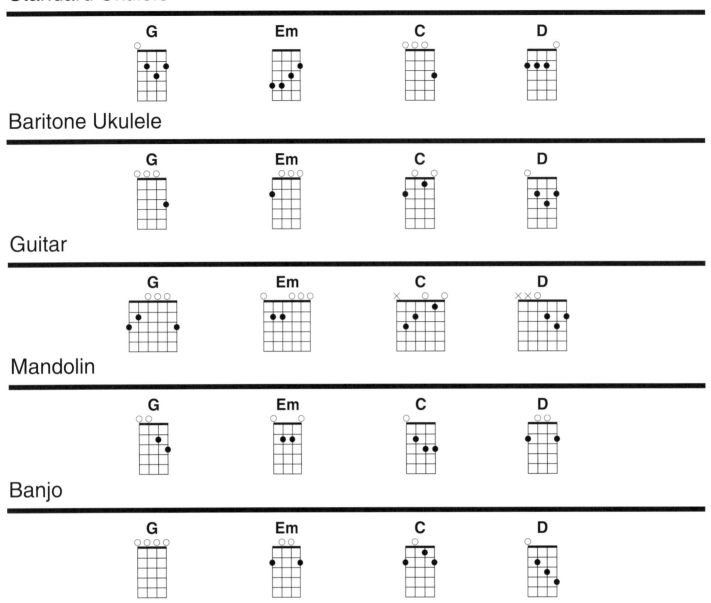

Big Spike Hammer

Words and Music by Bobby Osborne and Pete Goble

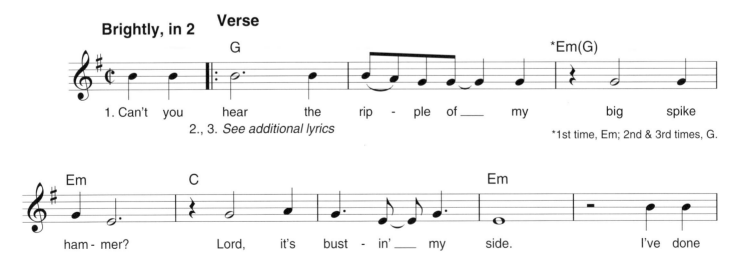

Brightly, in 2 **Verse**

G   *Em(G)

1. Can't you hear the rip - ple of ___ my big spike
2., 3. *See additional lyrics*

*1st time, Em; 2nd & 3rd times, G.

Em   C   Em

ham - mer? Lord, it's bust - in' ___ my side. I've done

2. I'm the best hammer swinger in this big section, gang.
   Big Bill Johnson is my name.
   This spike hammer that I swing for a dollar and a half a day,
   It's all for my Della Mae.

3. Well, I've been lots of places, not much I ain't done;
   There's still a lot of things I'd like to see.
   Big spike hammer that I swing, or the woman that I love,
   Yeah, one's gonna be the death of me.

Standard Ukulele

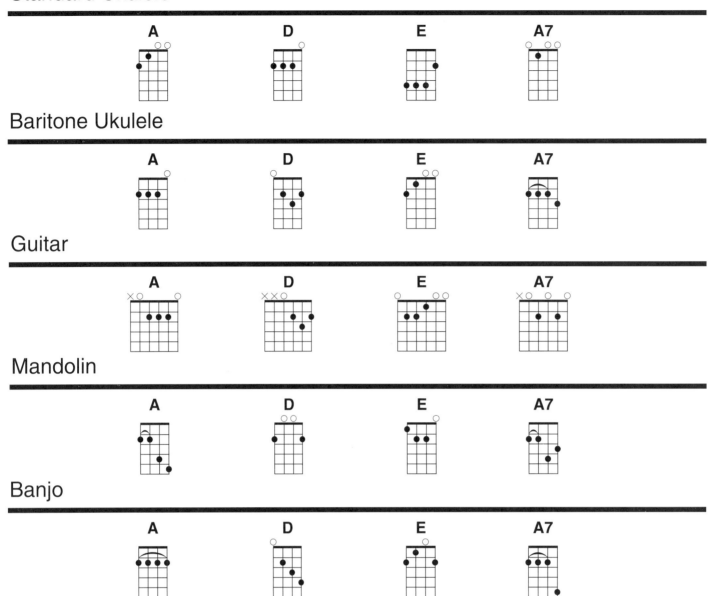

Baritone Ukulele

Guitar

Mandolin

Banjo

Blue Moon of Kentucky
Words and Music by Bill Monroe

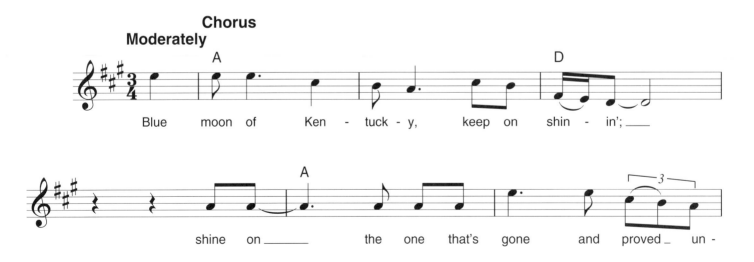

Chorus
Moderately

A   D

Blue   moon   of   Ken - tuck - y,   keep on   shin - in';

A

shine   on   the   one   that's   gone   and   proved   un -

Standard Ukulele

Baritone Ukulele

Guitar

Mandolin

Banjo

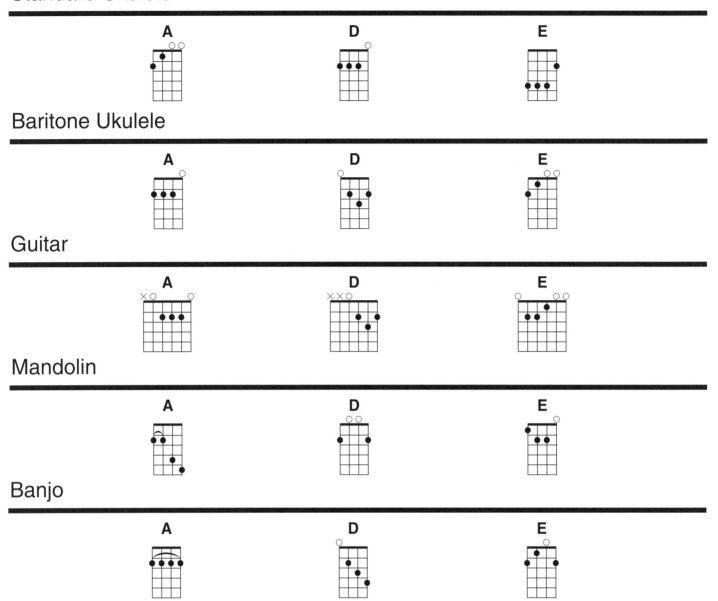

Blue Ridge Cabin Home

Words and Music by Louise Certain and Gladys Stacey

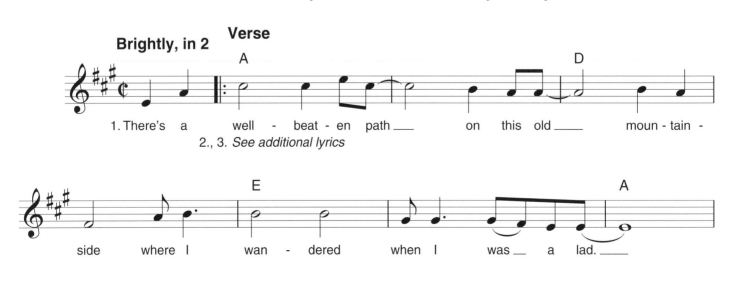

1. There's a well-beat-en path on this old mountain-side where I wan-dered when I was a lad.

2., 3. *See additional lyrics*

Additioinal Lyrics

2. Now my thoughts wander back to the ramshackle shack
   In those Blue Ridge hills far away.
   My mother and dad were laid there to rest;
   They are sleeping in peace together there.

3. I return to that old cabin home with a sigh;
   I've been longing for days gone by.
   When I die, won't you bury me on that old mountainside,
   Make my resting place upon the hill so high.

Standard Ukulele

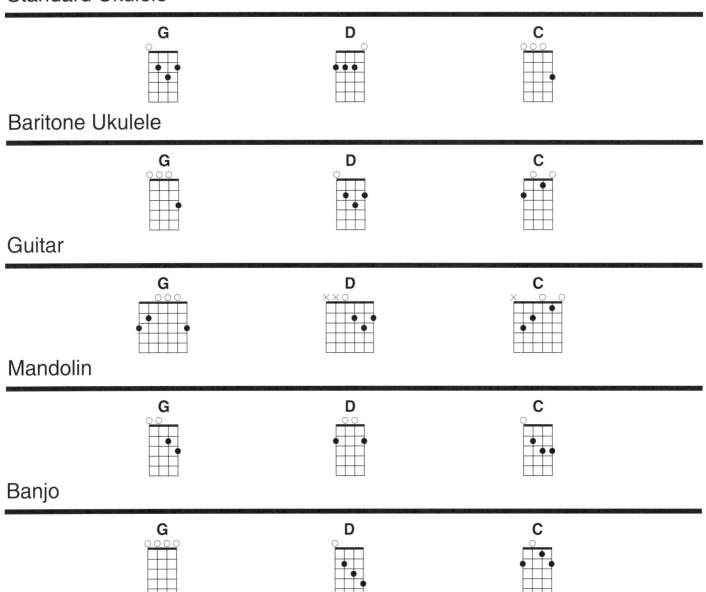

Baritone Ukulele

Guitar

Mandolin

Banjo

Blue Ridge Mountain Blues

Words and Music by Bill Clifton and Buddy Dee

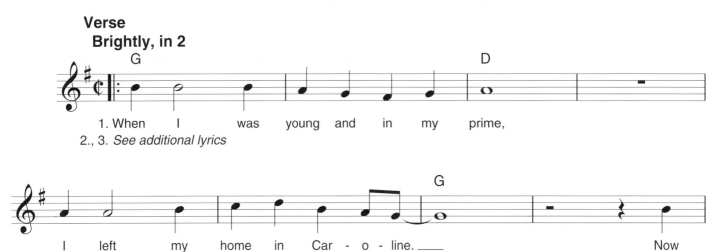

Verse
Brightly, in 2

1. When I was young and in my prime,
2., 3. *See additional lyrics*

I left my home in Car - o - line. ____ Now

Additional Lyrics

2. I see a window with a light,
I see two heads of snowy white.
It seems I hear them both recite:
"Where is my wand'ring boy tonight?"

3. I'm gonna do right by my pa,
I'm gonna do right by my ma.
I'll hang around the kitchen door;
No work or worry anymore.

Standard Ukulele

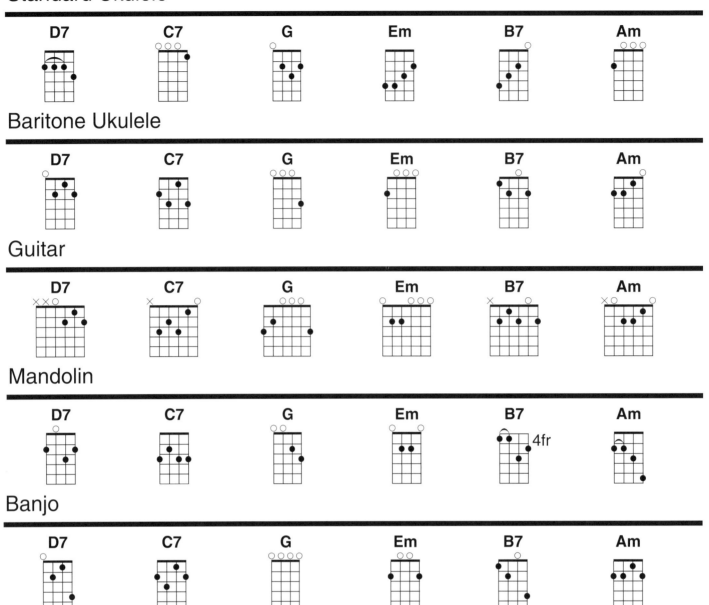

Baritone Ukulele

Guitar

Mandolin

Banjo

Blue Train
Words and Music by Dave Allen

Verse
Brightly, in 2

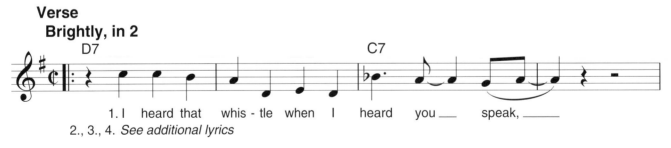

1. I heard that whis-tle when I heard you ___ speak, ___
2., 3., 4. *See additional lyrics*

felt that rum-ble un-der-neath my ___ feet.

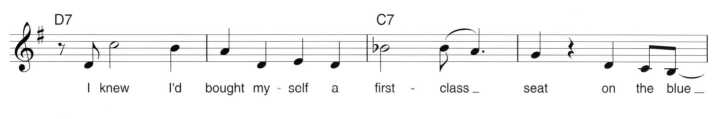

I knew I'd bought my-self a first - class __ seat on the blue __

__ train. __

Chorus

Blue train, blue train, bro - ken

hearts ride free on the blue train,

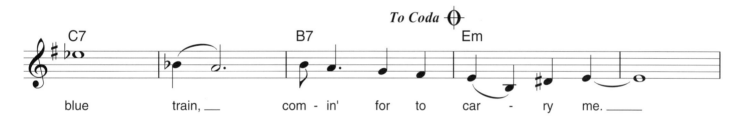

To Coda ✛

blue train, __ com - in' for to car - ry me. __

D.C. al Coda (take repeat)

✛ **Coda**

car - ry me __

on __ the blue __ train. __

Additional Lyrics

2. I knew you'd break me down and leave me flat.
   I saw it coming but I turned my back.
   I feel like a nickel on the railroad track.
   Here comes the blue train.

3. It's not the first time I've been down this line.
   I've done some travelin' with this heart of mine.
   Seems to be a longer ride each time
   On the blue train.

4. When I get home I'm gonna lock my heart,
   Try and tear away the wounded part.
   I'm gonna get myself a good head start
   And outrun the blue train.

Standard Ukulele

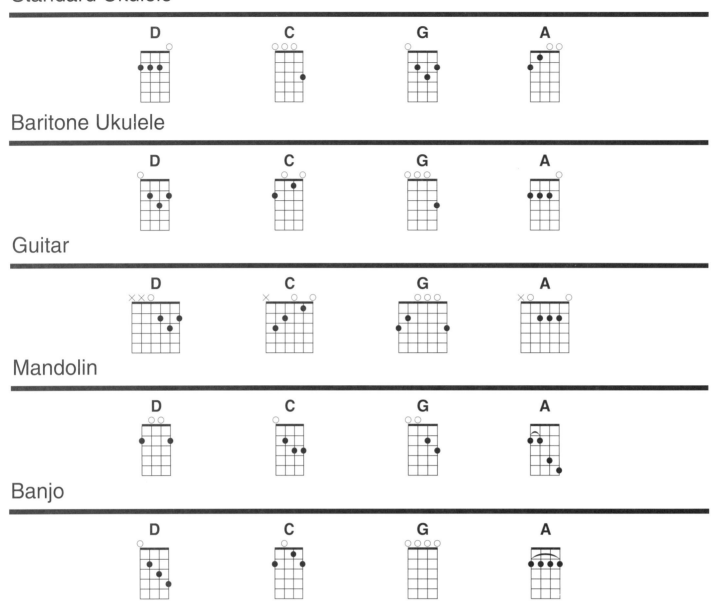

Baritone Ukulele

Guitar

Mandolin

Banjo

Bringing Mary Home

Words and Music by Chaw Mank, Joe Kingston and John Duffey

Verse
Moderately slow, in 2

1. I was driv - ing down _ a lone - ly road _ on a dark and storm - y
2.-5. *See additional lyrics*

night _____ when a lit - tle girl ___ by the

road - side showed up in my head - lights. I

stopped and she got in back, __ and in a shak - y

tone, she said, "My name __ is Mar - y. Please

won't __ you take __ me home?"

2. She
3. I
4. A
5. "But

Additional Lyrics

2. She must have been so frightened all alone there in the night.
There was something strange about her 'cause her face was deathly white.
She sat so pale and quiet in the back seat all alone.
I never will forget that night I took Mary home.

3. I pulled into the driveway where she told me to go.
Got out to help her from the car and opened up the door.
But I just could not believe my eyes 'cause the back seat was bare.
I looked all around the car but Mary wasn't there.

4. A light shone from the porch; someone opened up the door.
I asked about the little girl that I was looking for.
Then the lady gently smiled and brushed a tear away.
She said, "It sure was nice of you to go out of your way."

5. "But thirteen years ago today, in a wreck just down the road,
Our darling Mary lost her life and we miss her so.
Oh, thank you for your trouble and the kindness you have shown.
You're the thirteenth one who's been here bringing Mary home."

Standard Ukulele

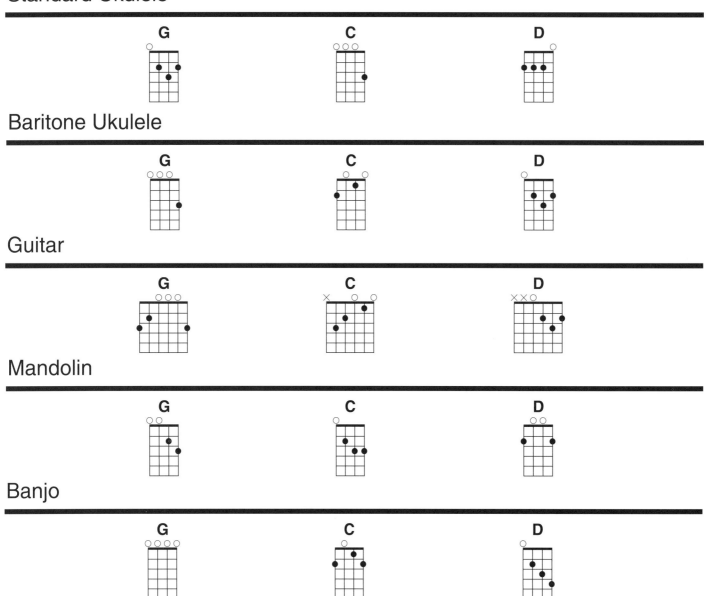

Baritone Ukulele

Guitar

Mandolin

Banjo

Bury Me Beneath the Willow
Traditional

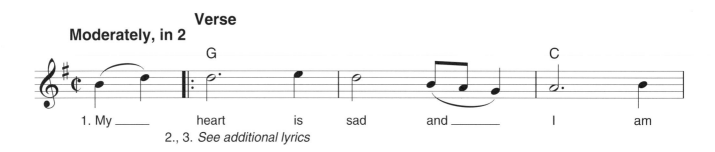

Moderately, in 2

Verse

G

C

1. My _____ heart is sad and _____ I am
2., 3. *See additional lyrics*

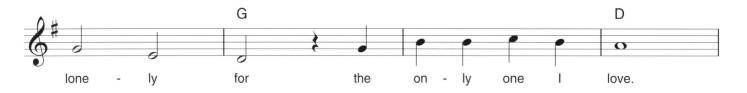

G

D

lone - ly for the on - ly one I love.

When ___ shall I see her, ___ oh no

nev - er, till we meet in heav - en a - bove.

Chorus

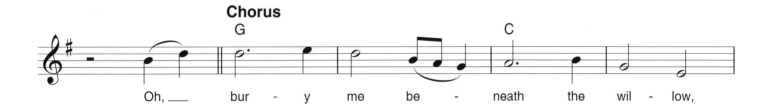

Oh, ___ bur - y me be - neath the wil - low,

un - der the weep - ing wil - low tree so ___

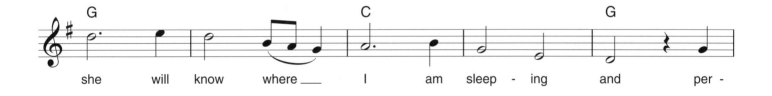

she will know where ___ I am sleep - ing and per -

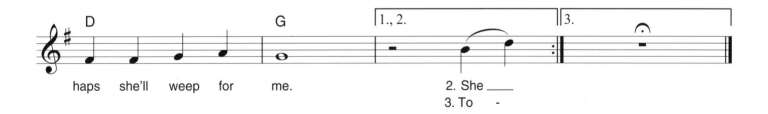

haps she'll weep for me. 2. She ___
3. To -

Additional Lyrics

2. She told me that she dearly loved me.
   How could I believe it untrue?
   Until the angels softly whispered,
   "She will prove untrue to you."

3. Tomorrow was our wedding day,
   Oh God, oh God, where can she be?
   She's out a-courting with another
   And no longer cares for me.

Standard Ukulele

Baritone Ukulele

Guitar

Mandolin

Banjo

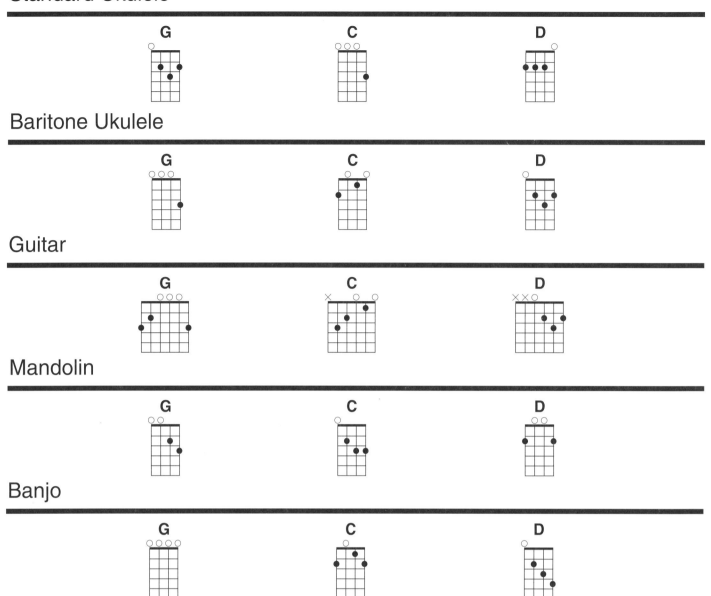

Can't You Hear Me Callin'
Words and Music by Bill Monroe

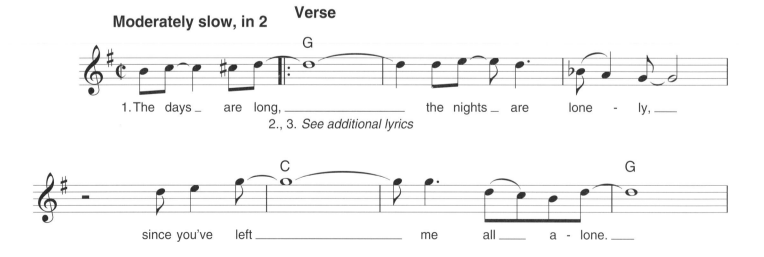

Moderately slow, in 2   **Verse**

1. The days _ are long, _____ the nights _ are lone - ly, _

2., 3. *See additional lyrics*

since you've left _____ me all _ a - lone. _

I loved you so, _____ my lit - tle dar - lin'.

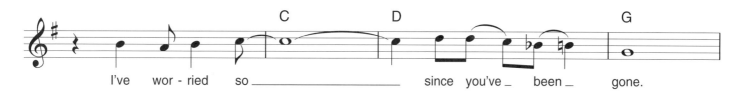

I've wor - ried so _____ since you've _ been _ gone.

Chorus

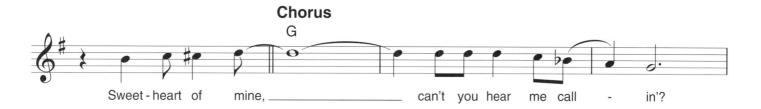

Sweet - heart of mine, _____ can't you hear me call - in'?

A mil - lion times, _____ I loved you best. __

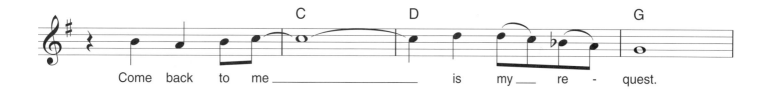

I mis - treat - ed you, _____ Lord, and I'm sor - ry.

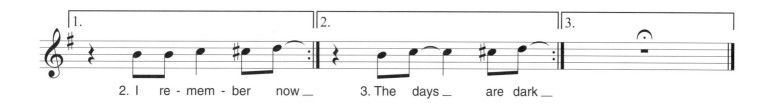

Come back to me _____ is my _ re - quest.

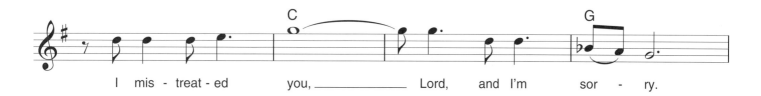

1.
2. I re - mem - ber now _

2.
3. The days _ are dark _

3.

Additional Lyrics

2. I remember now the night we parted.
   A big mistake has caused it all.
   If you'll return, sunshine will follow.
   To stay away would be my fall.

3. The days are dark, my little darlin'.
   Oh, how I need your sweet embrace.
   When I awoke the sun was shinin'.
   When I looked up, I saw your face.

Standard Ukulele

Baritone Ukulele

Guitar

Mandolin

Banjo

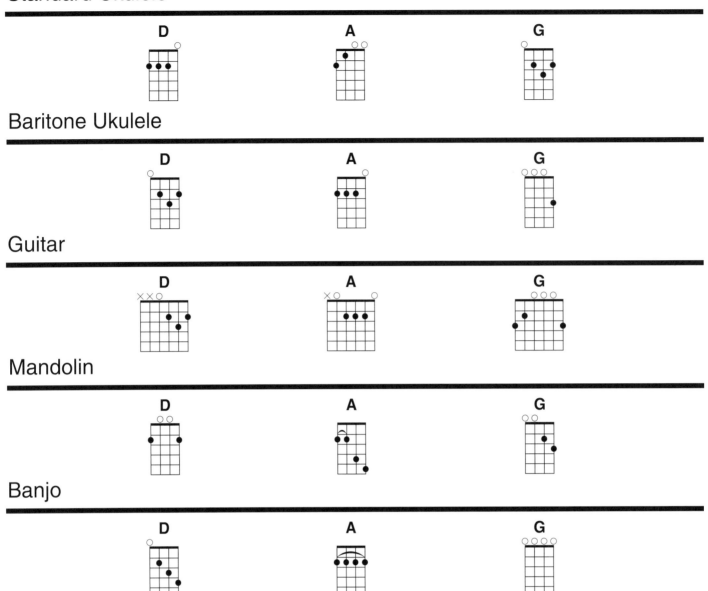

Cash on the Barrelhead
Words and Music by Charles Louvin and Ira Louvin

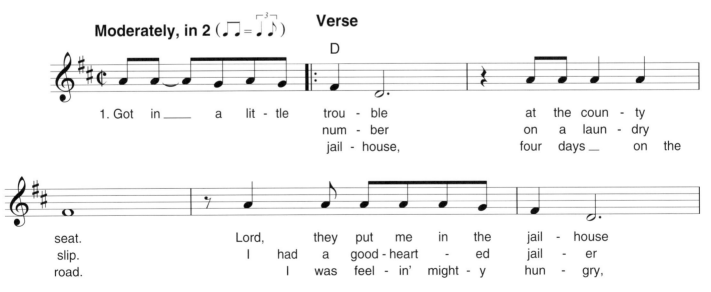

1. Got in a lit-tle trou-ble at the coun-ty
   num-ber on a laun-dry
   jail-house, four days on the

seat. Lord, they put me in the jail-house
slip. I had a good-heart-ed jail-er
road. I was feel-in' might-y hun-gry,

for   loaf - ing   on   the   street.   When the judge   heard the
with   a   six - gun   hip.   He   let   me   call   long ___
my   feet   a   heav - y   load.   Saw   a   Grey - hound ___

ver - dict, _____   I   was   a   guilt - y   man. _____
dis - tance; _____   she   said, __ "Num - ber,   please." _____
com - in', _____   stuck   up ___   my   thumb. _____

He   said,   "For - ty - five ___   dol - lars _____   or   thir - ty   day   in   the
And   no   soon - er   than   I   told   her, _____   she   shout - ed   out   at ___
Just   as   I   was   be - ing   seat - ed, _____   the   driv - er   caught   my ___

Chorus

can.   That - 'll   be   cash _____   on   the   bar - rel - head,
me,   "That - 'll   be   cash _____   on   the   bar - rel - head,
arm,   said, "That - 'll   be   cash _____   on   the   bar - rel - head,

son.   You   can   take   your   choice, _____   you're   twen - ty -
son.   Not   part,   not   half, _____   but   the   en - tire
son.   This   old ___   grey   dog _____   gets   paid ___   to

one.   No   mon - ey   down, _____   no   cred - it
sum.   No   mon - ey   down, _____   no   cred - it
run.   When   the   en - gine   starts _____   and   all   the   wheels   won't

plan.   No   time   to   chase _ you _____ 'cause I'm   a   bus - y
plan,   'cause   a   lit - tle   bird   tells _ me _____   you're   a   trav - el - in'
roll,   give   me   cash   on   the   bar - rel - head, _____   I'll   take   you   down _ the

1., 2.   3.

man."   2. Found   a   tel - e - phone _
man."   3. Thir - ty   days   in   the
road."

27

Standard Ukulele

Baritone Ukulele

Guitar

Mandolin

Banjo

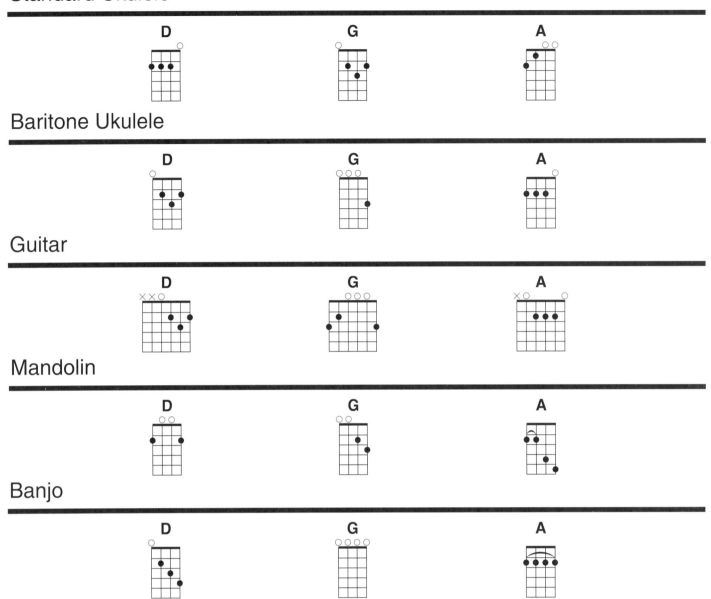

Cora Is Gone
Words and Music by Odell McLeod

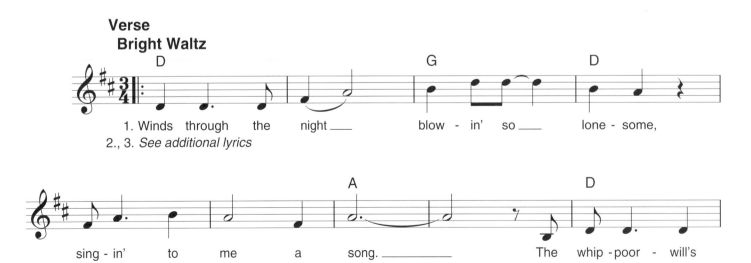

Verse
Bright Waltz

1. Winds through the night ___ blow - in' so ___ lone - some,
2., 3. *See additional lyrics*

sing - in' to me a song. ___ The whip - poor - will's

call ___ is just a re - mind - er pret - ty girls have

Chorus

hearts ___ made of stone. I wake with the blues ___ at

dawn. ___ My dar - lin' Cor - ey is

gone. I ___ don't know why ___ she

told me good - bye, ___ but my dar - lin' Cor - ey is

gone. 2. The

Additional Lyrics

2. The ring that she wears I bought for her finger,
   Purchased her raiment so fine.
   Gave her my last greenback dollar,
   And now she's left me behind.

3. Drifting along like a brush on a river,
   Caring not where I roam.
   Going to live in the deep forest;
   Dark hollow will be my new home.

Standard Ukulele

E   B7   E7   A

Baritone Ukulele

E   B7   E7   A

Guitar

E 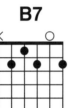   B7    E7   A

Mandolin

E   B7   E7   A

Banjo

E   B7   E7   A

The Crawdad Song
Traditional

Verse
Moderately, in 2

1. You get a line and I'll get a pole,
2. Get up, old man, you slept too late,
3. Get up, old wom-an, you slept too late,
4. What you gon-na do when the lake goes dry,

hon - ey. You get a line and
hon - ey. Get up, old man, and you
hon - ey. Get up, old wom-an, you
hon - ey? What you gon-na do when the

I'll get a pole, babe.
slept too late, babe.
slept too late, babe.
lake goes dry, babe?

You get a line and I'll get a pole, and
Get up, old man, you slept too late;
What you gon-na do when the lake goes dry? Sit

we'll go down to the craw-dad hole, hon - ey,
last piece of craw-dad's on your plate, hon - ey,
craw-dad man done passed your gate, hon - ey,
on the bank and watch the craw-dads die, hon - ey,

sug - ar ba - by, mine.

Play 4 times

Standard Ukulele

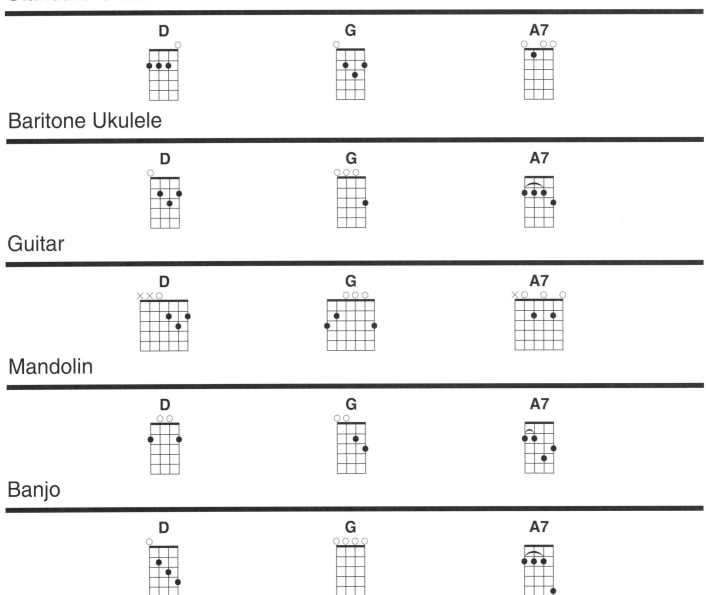

Baritone Ukulele

Guitar

Mandolin

Banjo

Cripple Creek

American Fiddle Tune

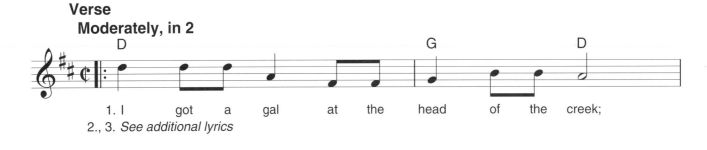

Verse
Moderately, in 2

D · · · · · · · · · · G · · · · D

1. I got a gal at the head of the creek;
2., 3. *See additional lyrics*

go up to see her 'bout the mid - dle of the week.

Kiss her on the mouth, just as sweet as an - y wine;

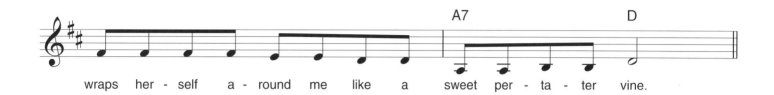

wraps her - self a - round me like a sweet per - ta - ter vine.

Chorus

Go - in' up Crip - ple Creek, go - in' in a run;

go - in' up Crip - ple Creek to have a lit - tle fun.

Go - in' up Crip - ple Creek, go - in' in a whirl;

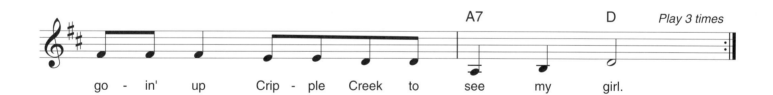

go - in' up Crip - ple Creek to see my girl.

Additional Lyrics

2. Girls on the Cripple Creek 'bout half grown;
   Jump on a boy like a dog on a bone.
   Roll my mouth, britches up to my knees;
   I'll wade old Cripple Creek when I please.

3. Cripple Creek's wide and Cripple Creek's deep;
   I'll wade old Cripple Creek afore I sleep.
   Roads are rocky and the hillside's muddy,
   And I'm so drunk that I can't stand studdy.

Standard Ukulele

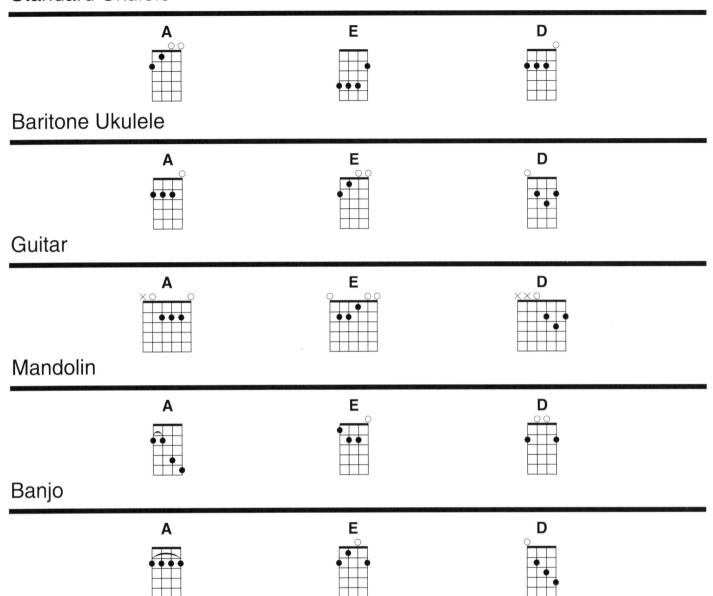

Baritone Ukulele

Guitar

Mandolin

Banjo

Dark Hollow
Words and Music by Bill Browning

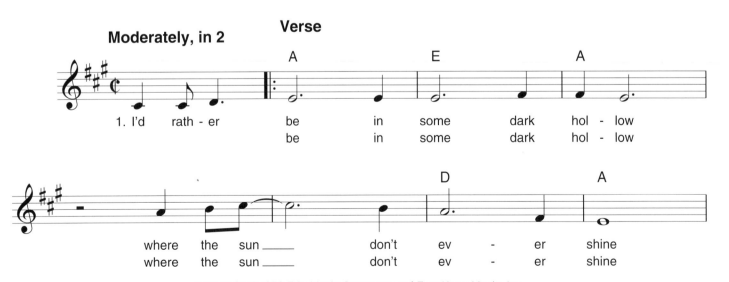

than   to   be _____   in   some   big ____

than   to   be _____   at   home   a - lone,   just ____

cit - y _____   in   a   small   room __ with

know - ing that __ you're gone; __   it   would   cause   me __ to

Chorus

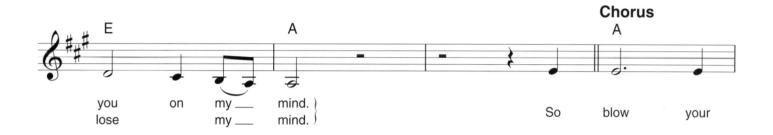

you   on   my __ mind.

lose   my __ mind.   So   blow   your

whis - tle,   freight   train.   Car - ry   me   far -   ther   on __

down   the   track. __   I'm   go - ing __ a - way; _

__   I'm   leav - ing   to - day. __   I'm   go - ing   but   I

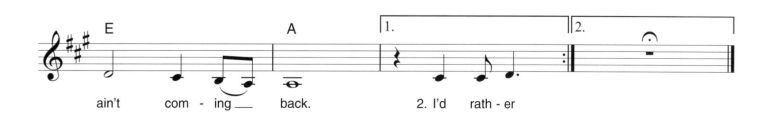

ain't   com - ing __ back.   2. I'd rath - er

Standard Ukulele

Baritone Ukulele

Guitar

Mandolin

Banjo

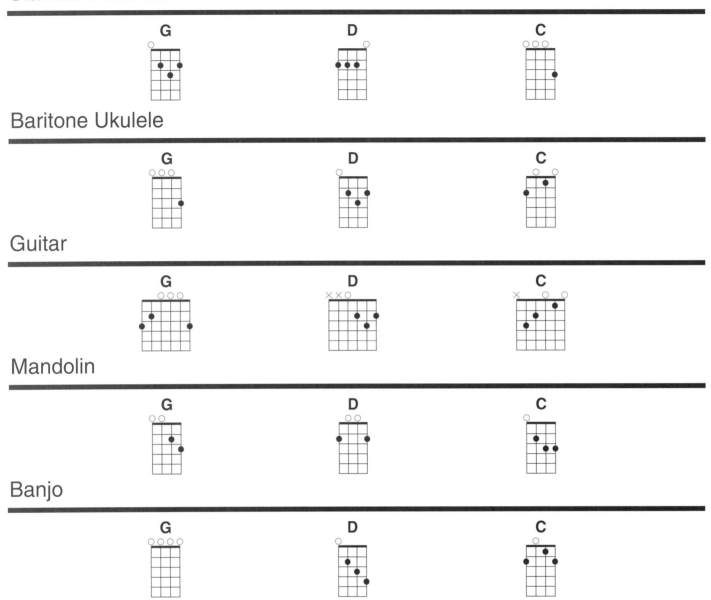

Doin' My Time

Words and Music by Jimmie Skinner

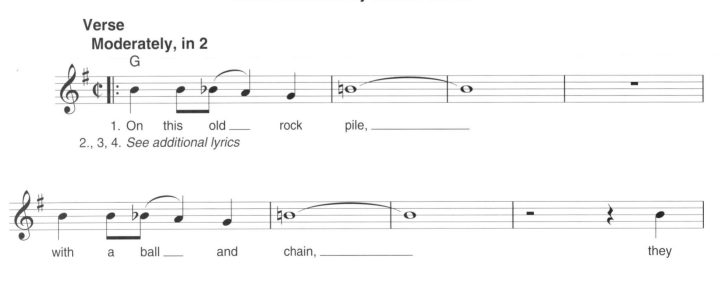

Verse
Moderately, in 2

G

1. On this old ___ rock pile, ___
2., 3., 4. *See additional lyrics*

with a ball ___ and chain, ___ they

call me by ____ a num - ber, not ____ a name, ____ Lord,

Lord.   Got - ta do ____ my time, _____

____ got - ta do ____ my time, _____

____ with an ach - ing heart _____

Play 4 times

and a wor - ried mind. _____

Additional Lyrics

2. When that old judge looked down and smiled,
   Said, "I'll put you in that good road for a while," Lord, Lord.
   Gotta do my time, gotta do my time
   With an aching heart and a worried mind.

3. You can hear my hammer, you can hear my song.
   I'm gonna swing it like John Henry all day long, Lord, Lord.
   Gotta do my time, gotta do my time
   With an aching heart and a worried mind.

4. It won't be long, just a few more days.
   I'll settle down and quit my rowdy ways, Lord, Lord,
   With that gal of mine, with that gal of mine.
   She'll be waiting for me when I've done my time.

Standard Ukulele

Baritone Ukulele

Guitar

Mandolin

Banjo

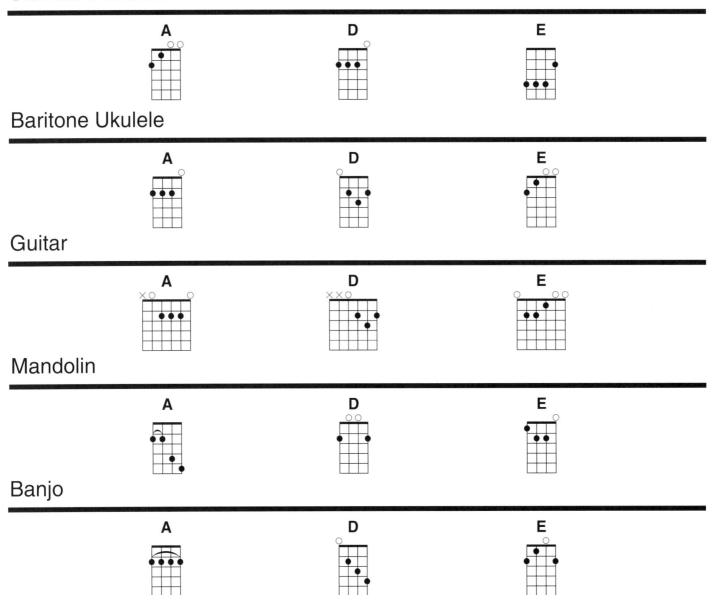

Dooley

Words by Mitchell F. Jayne
Music by Rodney Dillard

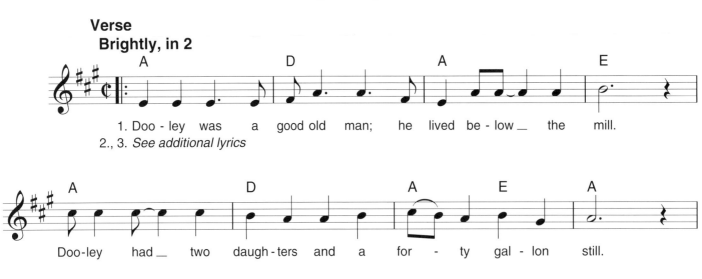

One gal watched the boil - er, the oth - er watched the spout, and

Ma - ma caught the bot - tles when old Doo - ley fetched them out. ____

Chorus

Doo - ley, slip - pin' up the hol - ler, Doo - ley,

try–in' to make a dol - lar. Doo - ley, give me a swal - ler and I'll

pay you back ___ some day. The

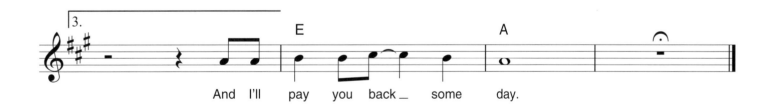

And I'll pay you back ___ some day.

Additional Lyrics

2. The revenuers came for him, slippin' though the woods,
   But Dooley kept behind them all and never lost his goods.
   Dooley was a trader when into town he'd come.
   Sugar by the bushel and molasses by the drum.

3. I remember very well the day old Dooley died.
   The women folk weren't sorry and the men stood around and cried.
   Now Dooley's on the mountain; he lies there all alone.
   They put a jug beside him and a barrel for his stone.

Standard Ukulele

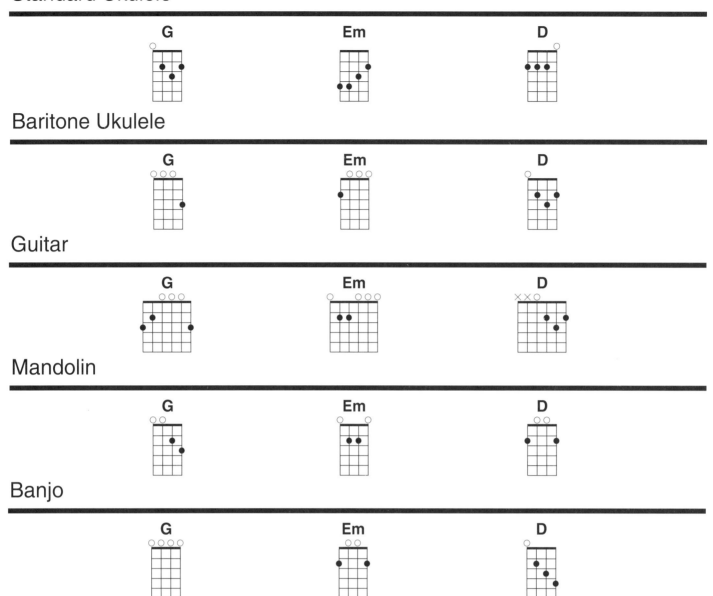

Baritone Ukulele

Guitar

Mandolin

Banjo

Down the Road
By Lester Flatt and Earl Scruggs

Verse

1. Now, down the road — just a mile or two —
2.-7. *See additional lyrics*

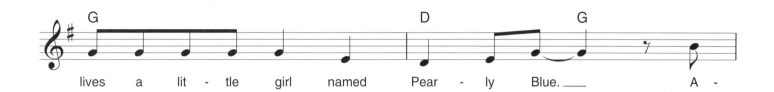

lives a lit - tle girl named Pear - ly Blue. — A -

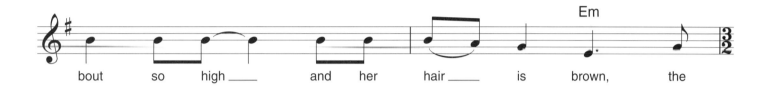

bout so high ——— and her hair ——— is brown, the

pret - ti - est thing, — boys, in this town.

Play 7 times

Additional Lyrics

2. Now, any time you want to know
Where I'm going down the road,
Get my girl on the line;
You'll find me there most any old time.

3. Now, every day and Sunday too
I go to see my Pearly Blue.
Before you hear that rooster crow,
You'll see me headed down the road.

4. Now, old man Flatt, he owned the farm
From the hog lot to the barn,
From the barn to the rail.
He made his living by carrying the mail.

5. Now, every time I get the blues
I walk the soles right off my shoes.
I don't know why I love her so;
That gal of mine lives down the road.

6. Now, down the road just a mile or two
Lives a little girl named Pearly Blue.
About so high and her hair is brown,
The prettiest thing, boys, in this town.

7. Now, every time I get the blues
I walk the soles right off my shoes.
I don't know why I love her so;
That gal of mine lives down the road.

Standard Ukulele

Baritone Ukulele

Guitar

Mandolin

Banjo

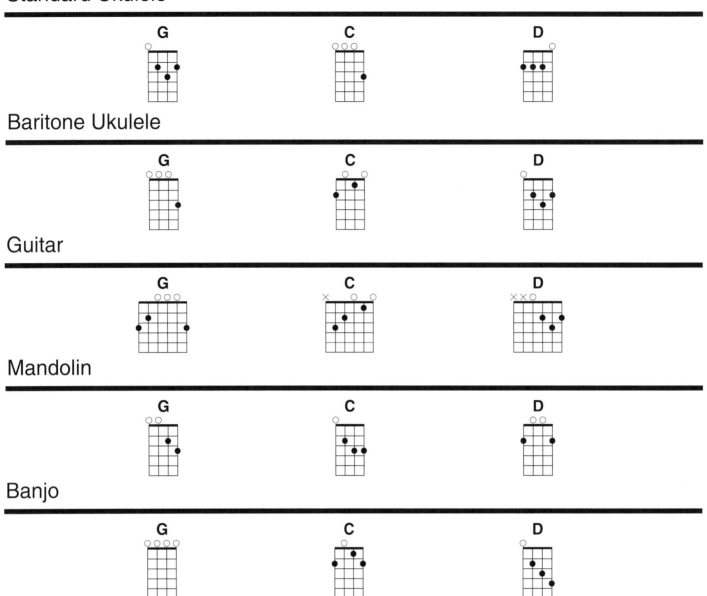

Foggy Mountain Top

Words and Music by A.P. Carter, Maybelle Carter and Sara Carter

𝄋 **Chorus**

Brightly, in 2

If I was on some ___ fog - gy moun - tain

top, I'd sail a - way to the west.

Additional Lyrics

2. Whenever you see that girl of mine,
   There's something you can tell her:
   She need not to fool her time away
   Just to court some other feller.

3. She caused me to weep and she caused me to mourn,
   She caused me to leave my home.
   To them lonesome pines and those good old times,
   I'm on my way back home.

4. Whenever you go a-courtin', boys,
   Let me tell you how to do:
   Pull off that long-tail roustabout;
   Put on your navy blue.

Standard Ukulele

Baritone Ukulele

Guitar

Mandolin

Banjo

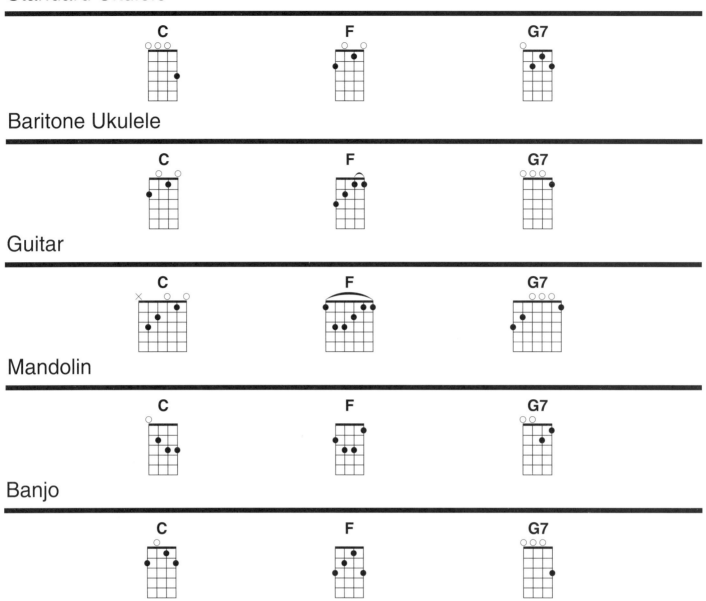

Footprints in the Snow

Words and Music by Rupert Jones

Verse
Moderately bright, in 2

1. Some folks like the sum - mer - time ____ when they can walk a -
2., 3. *See additional lyrics*

bout. Stroll - ing through the mead - ow green ____ is

Additional Lyrics

2. I dropped in to see her; there was a big round moon.
   Her mother said she just stepped out but'd be returning soon.
   I found her little footprints and I traced them through the snow,
   And I found her when the snow was on the ground.

3. Now she's up in heaven; she's with the angel band.
   I know I'm going to meet her in that promised land.
   But every time the snow falls, it brings back memories,
   For I found her when the snow was on the ground.

Standard Ukulele

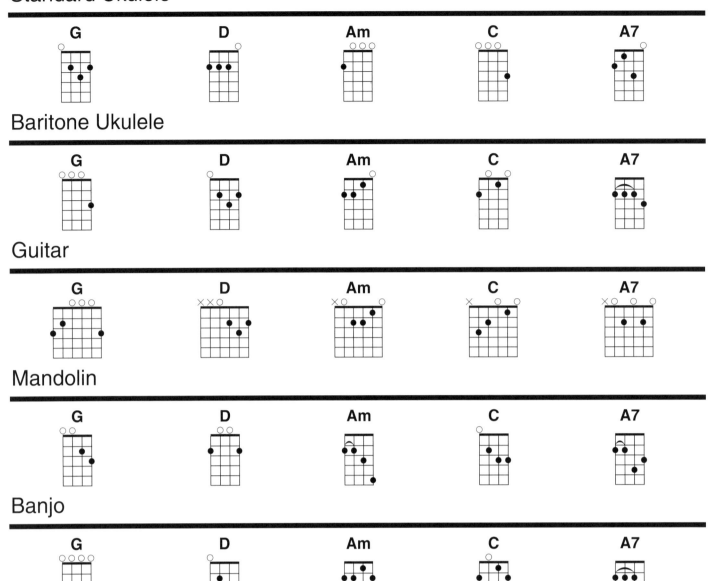

Baritone Ukulele

Guitar

Mandolin

Banjo

Fox on the Run
Words and Music by Tony Hazzard

%Chorus
Moderately, in 2

G — D — Am

She walks through the corn lead - ing down to the

C — Am — D — C

riv - er. Her hair shone like gold __ in the hot morn - ing

sun. _____ She took all the love that a

poor boy could give her and left me to die ____ like a

fox on the run, _____ like a fox, ____ like a fox, _

____ like a fox, ____ like a fox _____ on the run.

Verse

Fine

1. Now, ev - 'ry - bod - y knows _ the rea - son for the fall, ____
2. We'll pour a glass _ of wine ___ to for - ti - fy our souls. ___

___ when wom - an tempt - ed man _____ down in par - a - dise - 's
___ We'll talk a - bout the world ____ and friends we used _ to

hall. This wom - an tempt - ed me _____ and
know. I see a string of girls ____ who'll

took me for a ride. ___ Now like a lone - ly fox, ___ I
put me on the floor. ___ The game is near - ly o - ver and the

D.S. al Fine

need a place _ to hide. ___ She She
hounds are at ___ my door. ___

47

Standard Ukulele

Baritone Ukulele

Guitar

Mandolin

Banjo

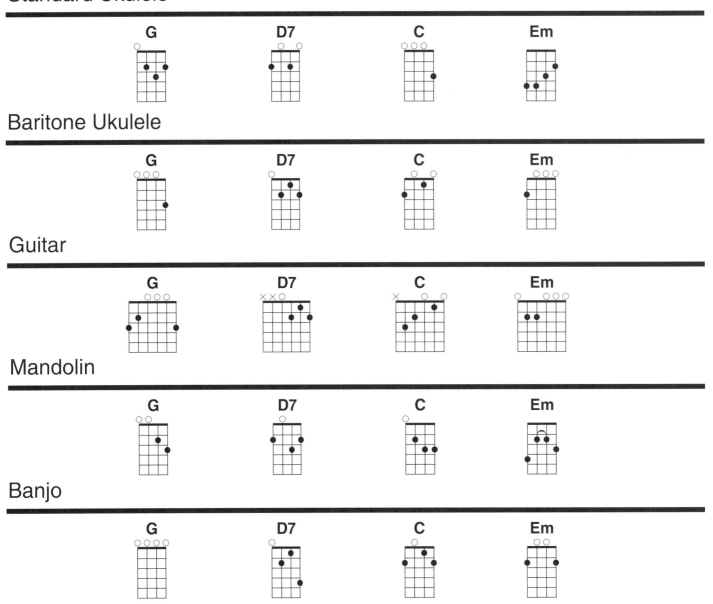

Hand Me Down My Walking Cane

Words and Music by James A. Bland

Verse
Moderately, in 2

1. Hand me down _____ my walk-ing cane, _____ hand me
2.-7. *See additional lyrics*

down _____ my walk-ing cane, _____ oh, hand me down my

walk - ing cane; I'm - a gon - na leave on that mid - night train 'cause

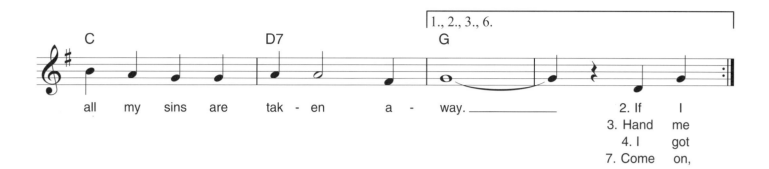

1., 2., 3., 6.

all my sins are tak - en a - way. _____ 2. If I
3. Hand me
4. I got
7. Come on,

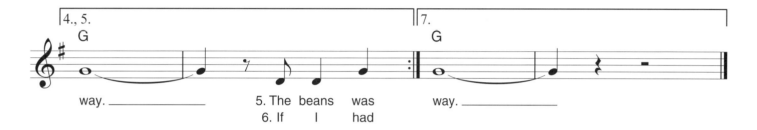

4., 5. / **7.**

way. _____ 5. The beans was / way. _____
6. If I had

Additional Lyrics

2. If I die in Tennessee,
   If I die in Tennessee,
   Oh, if I die in Tennessee,
   Just send me back by COD
   'Cause all my sins are taken away.

3. Hand me down my bottle of corn,
   Hand me down my bottle of corn,
   Oh, hand me down my bottle of corn;
   I'm gonna get drunk as sure as you're born
   'Cause all my sins are taken away.

4. I got drunk and I got in jail,
   I got drunk and I got in jail,
   Oh, I got drunk and I got in jail,
   And I had no one to go my bail
   'Cause all my sins are taken away.

5. The beans was tough and the meat was fat,
   The beans was tough and the meat was fat,
   Oh, the beans was tough and the meat was fat,
   And oh, my Lord, I couldn't eat that
   'Cause all my sins are taken away.

6. If I had listened to what Mama said,
   If I had listened to what Mama said,
   Oh, if I had listened to what Mama said
   I'd-a been a-sleeping on a feather bed
   'Cause all my sins are taken away.

7. Come on, Mama, and go my bail,
   Come on, Mama, and go my bail,
   Oh, come on, Mama, and go my bail
   And get me out of this buggy jail
   'Cause all my sins are taken away.

Standard Ukulele

Baritone Ukulele

Guitar

Mandolin

Banjo

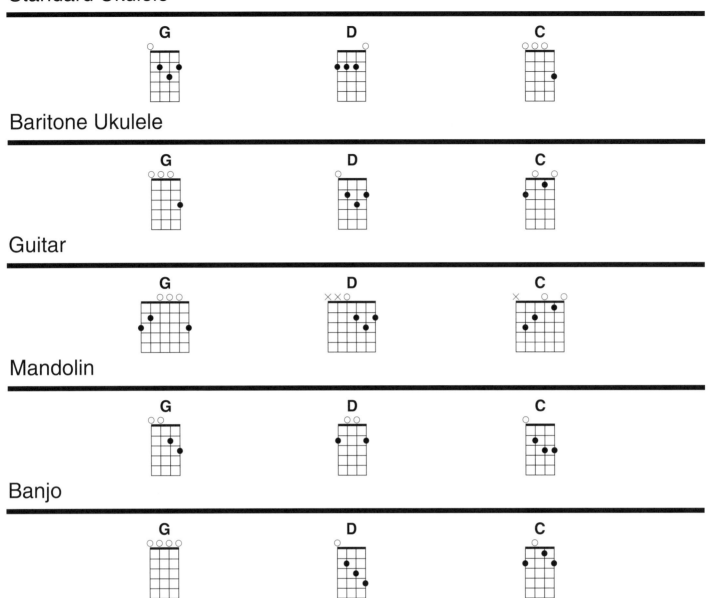

Head Over Heels in Love with You
(I'm Head Over Heels in Love)
Words and Music by Lester Flatt

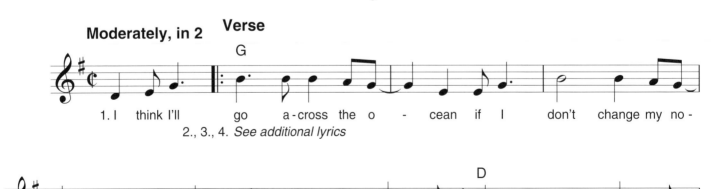

Moderately, in 2   **Verse**

1. I think I'll go a-cross the o - cean if I don't change my no -
2., 3., 4. *See additional lyrics*

— tion; I've just got to for - get you if I can.

Oh, I'm feel - in' so blue, ____ I

don't know what to do, for I'm head o - ver

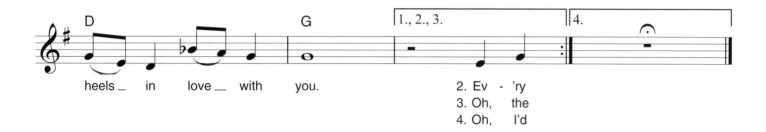

heels _ in love _ with you.

2. Ev - 'ry
3. Oh, the
4. Oh, I'd

Additional Lyrics

2. Every day is sad and lonely
For I'm thinking of you only.
Oh, I just can't sleep when I lay down.
Oh, I'm feeling so blue,
I don't know what to do,
For I'm head over heels in love with you.

3. Oh, the nights are long and dreary;
All I do is sit and worry.
I just can't bear the thought of losing you.
Oh, I'm feeling so blue,
I don't know what to do,
For I'm head over heels in love with you.

4. Oh, I'd like to be forgiven
But this life ain't worth livin'
If have to sit and worry over you.
Oh, I'm feeling so blue,
I don't know what to do,
For I'm head over heels in love with you.

Standard Ukulele

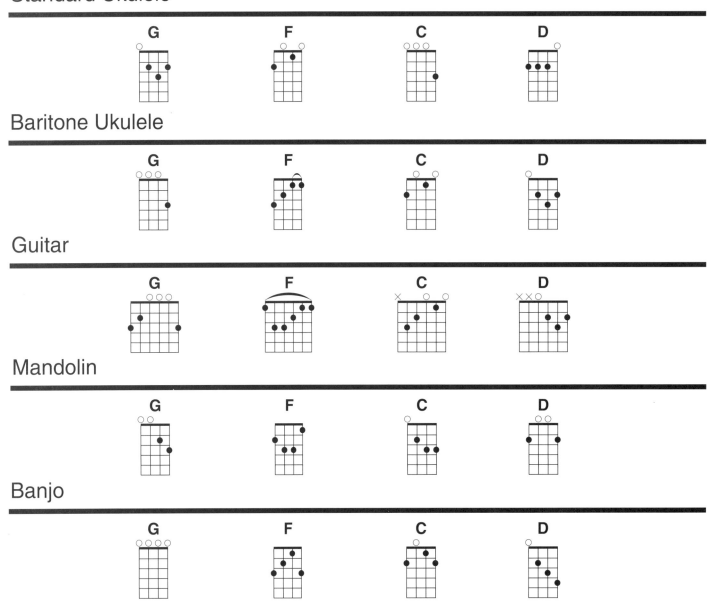

Baritone Ukulele

Guitar

Mandolin

Banjo

High on a Mountain Top

Words and Music by Ola Belle Reed

Chorus
Moderately, in 2

High on a moun-tain-top, __ stand-ing all a-lone, __

__ won-d'ring where the years __ of my life have flown.

Standard Ukulele

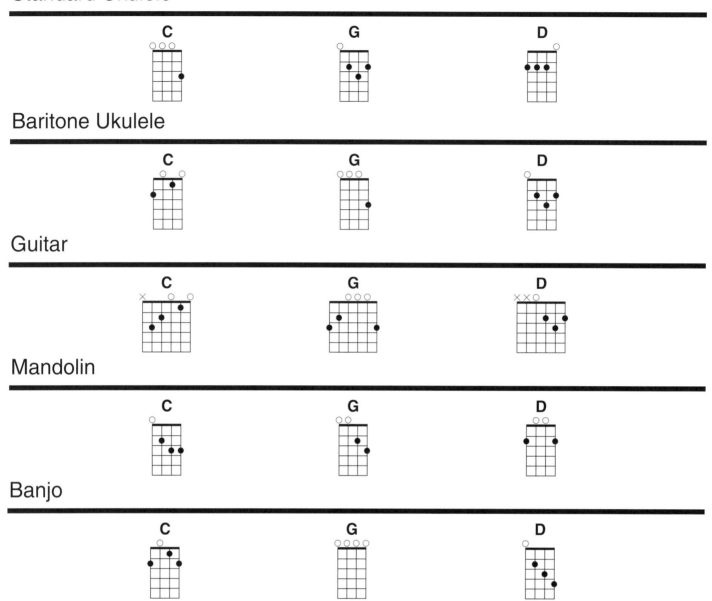

Baritone Ukulele

Guitar

Mandolin

Banjo

How Mountain Girls Can Love

Words and Music by Carter Stanley

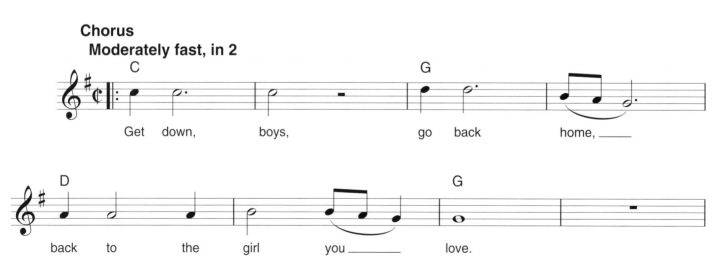

Chorus
Moderately fast, in 2

Get down, boys, go back home, ____

back to the girl you ____ love.

55

Standard Ukulele

Baritone Ukulele

Guitar

Mandolin

Banjo

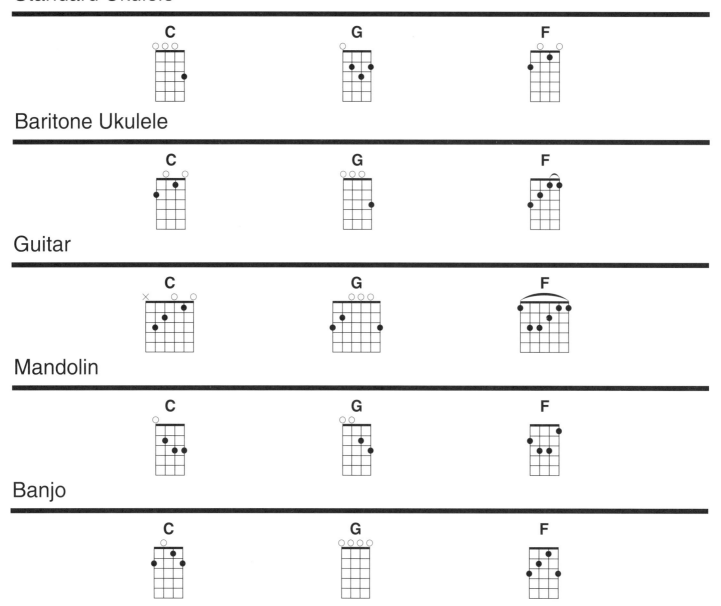

I Ain't Goin' to Work Tomorrow

Words and Music by A.P. Carter, Lester Flatt and Earl Scruggs

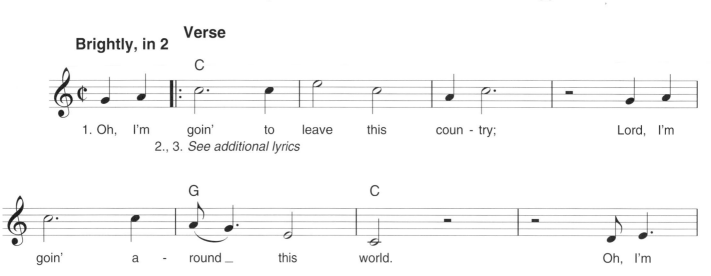

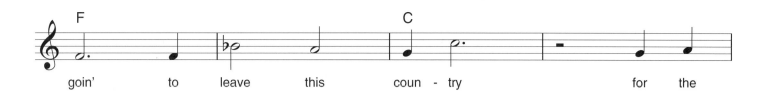

goin'   to   leave   this   coun - try   for   the

sake   of   one __   lit - tle   girl.   Oh,   I

Chorus

ain't goin'   to   work   to - mor - row;   I   ain't goin'   to

work __   next __   day.   Lord,   I   ain't   goin'   to

work   to - mor - row,   for   it   may   be   a

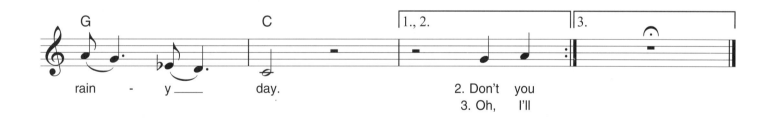

rain - y ____   day.   2. Don't   you
                                                         3. Oh,   I'll

Additional Lyrics

2. Don't you hear my banjo ringing,
   Don't you hear that mournful sound.
   Don't you hear those pretty girls laughing,
   Standing on the cold, cold ground.

3. Oh, I'll hang my head in sorrow;
   Lord, I'll hang my head and cry.
   Oh, I'll hang my head in sorrow
   As my darling passes by.

Standard Ukulele

Baritone Ukulele

Guitar

Mandolin

Banjo

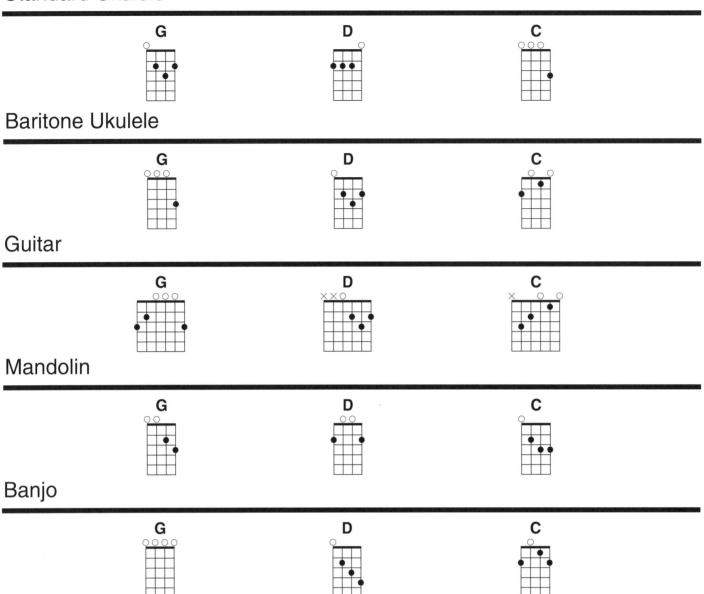

I Am a Man of Constant Sorrow
Words and Music by Carter Stanley and Ralph Stanley

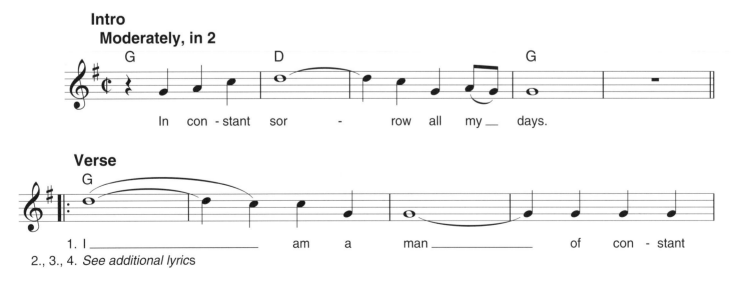

2., 3., 4. *See additional lyrics*

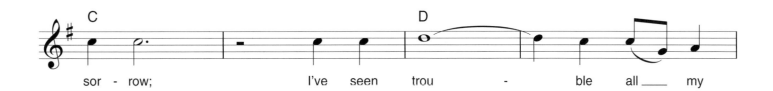

sor - row; I've seen trou - ble all ___ my

days. I _____ bid fare -

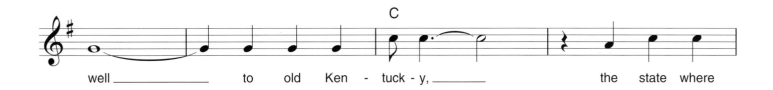

well _____ to old Ken - tuck - y, _____ the state where

I _____ was borned and ___ raised. (The state where

he _____ was borned and ___ raised.)

Additional Lyrics

2. For six long years I've been in trouble;
   No pleasure here on earth I find,
   For in this world I'm bound to ramble.
   I have no friends to help me now.
   (He has no friends to help him now.)

3. You can bury me in some deep valley
   For many years where I may lay.
   Then you may learn to love another
   While I am sleeping in my grave.
   (While he is sleeping in his grave.)

4. Maybe your friends think I'm just a stranger;
   My face you'll never will see no more.
   But there is one promise that is given:
   I'll meet you on God's golden shore.
   (He'll meet you on God's golden shore.)

Standard Ukulele

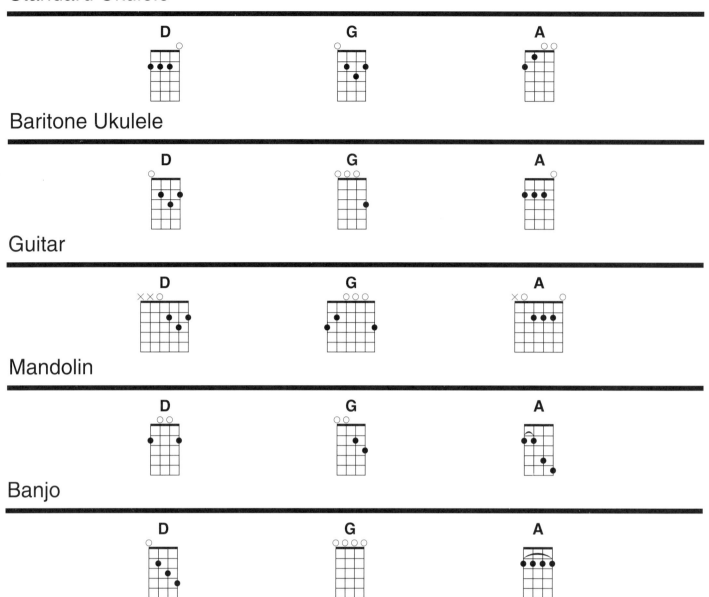

Baritone Ukulele

Guitar

Mandolin

Banjo

I Wonder Where You Are Tonight

Words and Music by Johnny Bond

Verse
Moderately, in 2

1. Now to - night I'm sad; my heart is wea - ry. I'm

2., 3. *See additional lyrics*

won - d'ring if I'm wrong or right to

dream a - bout you though you've left me. I

won - der where you are to - night. The

Chorus

rain is cold and slow - ly fall - ing up -

on my win - dow - pane to - night, and though your

love is e - ven cold - er, I won - der

where you are to - night.

1., 2.
3.

2. Your
3. Then

Additional Lyrics

2. Your heart was cold, you never loved me,
   Though you often said you cared.
   And now you've gone to find another,
   Someone who knows the love I shared.

3. Then came the dawn the day you left me;
   I tried to smile with all my might.
   But you could see the pain within me
   That lingers in my heart tonight.

Standard Ukulele

Baritone Ukulele

Guitar

Mandolin

Banjo

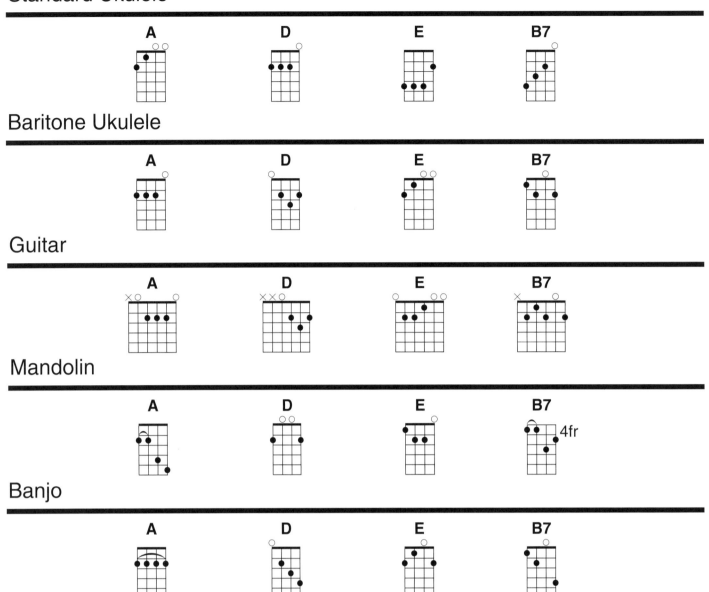

I'm Blue, I'm Lonesome

Words and Music by Bill Monroe and Hank Williams

1. The lone - some sigh _____ of a train go - ing by _____ makes me want to stop and cry. _____

I re-call the day _____ it took _____ you a-way. _____ I'm blue, I'm lone-some too. _____

𝄌 Chorus

When _____ I hear _____ the whis-tle blow, _____ I want to pack my clothes _____ and go. _____ The lone-some sigh _____ of a train go-ing by _____ makes me want to stop and cry. _____ 2. In the

Verse

still of the night, _____ in the pale moon-light, _ the winds, they moan and cry. _____ These lone-some blues _____ I _____ just can't lose. _ I'm blue, I'm lone-some too. _____

Standard Ukulele

Baritone Ukulele

Guitar

Mandolin

Banjo

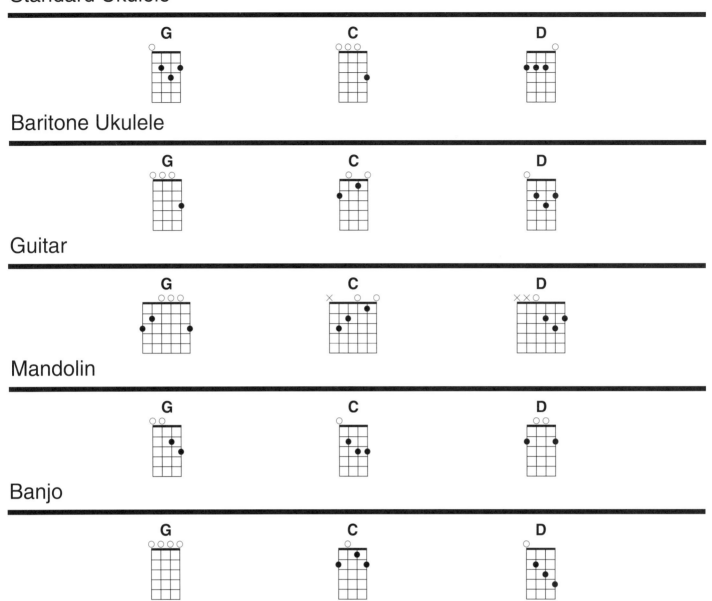

If I Lose
Words and Music by Ralph Stanley

Verse
Moderately, in 2

G

1. I nev-er thought I'd need _ you, but now I find I'm wrong. _

D   G

Come on back, _ sweet ma-ma, back where you be-long.   I've

Chorus

gam - bled o - ver town, find that I ___ can't win.

Come on back ___ and pick me up a - gain. ___ Now, if I

lose, let me lose. ___ I don't care _____
(If I lose) (let me lose) ___ (I don't

___ how much I ___ lose. If I lose a hun - dred
care how much I lose.)

dol - lars while I'm try - in' to win a dime, ___ my ba - by, she's ___ got

Verse

Fine

mon - ey all ___ the time. 2. Of all the oth - er gals ___

___ I know, none can take ___ your place, ___ 'cause when I get in -

to a jam, ___ they just ___ ain't in the race. So now that you're back, ___

___ dear, let's make an - oth - er round. ___ With you ___ here by my

D.S. al Fine

side, babe, my deal just can't ___ go down. Now if I

65

Standard Ukulele

Baritone Ukulele

Guitar

Mandolin

Banjo

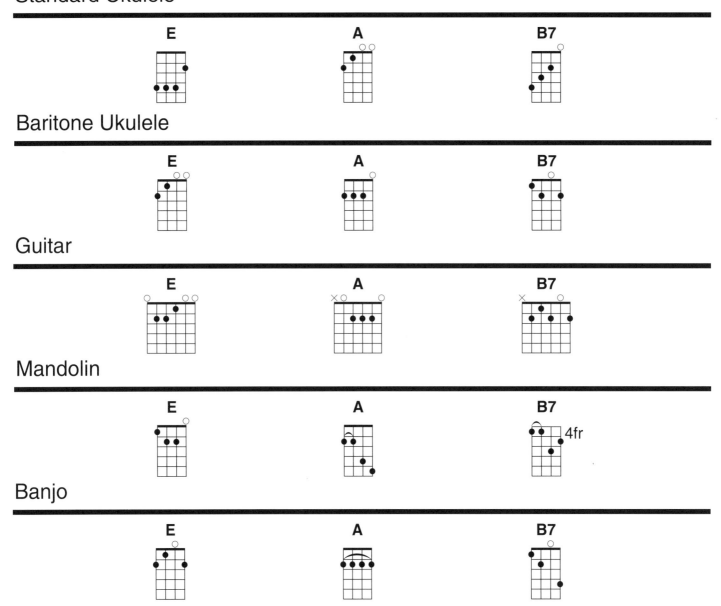

In the Pines

Words and Music by Thomas Bryant, Jimmie Davis and Clayton McMichen

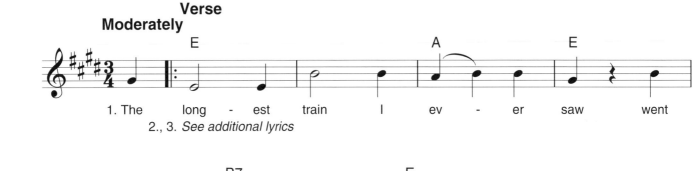

1. The long - est train I ev - er saw went

2., 3. *See additional lyrics*

down that ___ Geor - gia ___ line. The

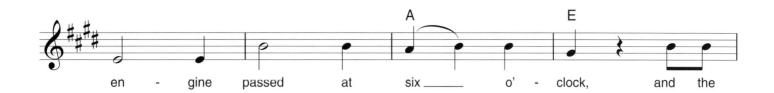

en - gine passed at six _____ o' - clock, and the

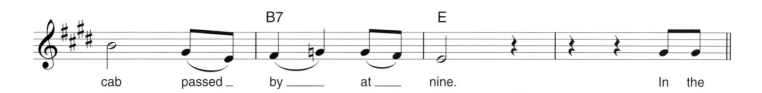

cab passed _ by _____ at _____ nine. In the

Chorus

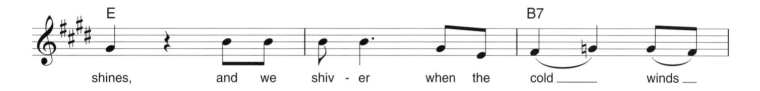

pines, in the pines, where the sun _____ nev - er

shines, and we shiv - er when the cold _____ winds _

blow.   2. I   3. Lit - tle

Additional Lyrics

2. I asked my captain for the time of day;
   He said he throwed his watch away.
   A long steel rail and a short crosstie,
   I'm on my way back home.

3. Little girl, little girl, what have I done
   That makes you treat me so?
   You caused me to weep, you caused me to moan;
   You caused me to leave my home.

Standard Ukulele

Baritone Ukulele

Guitar

Mandolin

Banjo

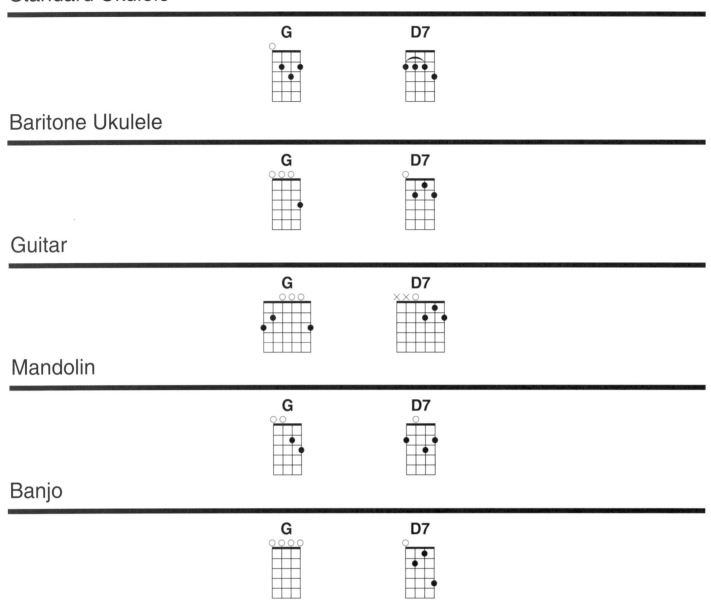

Jimmie Brown the Newsboy
Words and Music by A.P. Carter

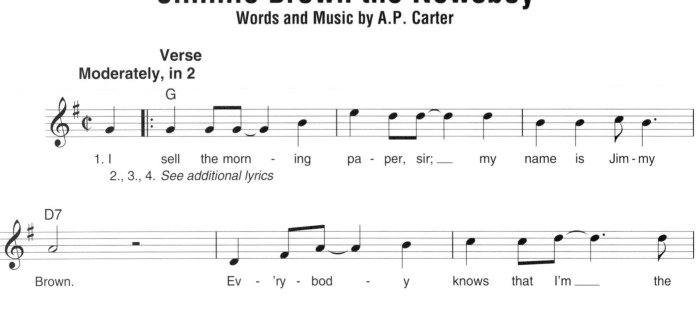

Verse
Moderately, in 2

G

1. I   sell   the   morn - ing   pa - per, sir; __ my   name   is   Jim - my
2., 3., 4. *See additional lyrics*

D7

Brown.   Ev - 'ry - bod - y   knows   that   I'm __ the

news - boy of the town. ___ You can hear me yell - ing

"Morn - ing Star," ___ run - ning a - long the street.

Got no hat up - on ___ my head, ___ no shoes ___ up - on ___ my

feet.

3. My
4. I

Additional Lyrics

2. Never mind, sir, how I look; don't look at me and frown.
   I sell the morning paper, sir; my name is Jimmie Brown.
   I'm awful cold and hungry, sir; my coat is mighty thin.
   I wander about from place to place, my daily bread to win.

3. My father died a drunkard, sir, I've heard my mother say.
   I am helping mother, sir, as I journey on my way.
   My mother always tells me, sir, I've nothing in the world to lose.
   I'll get a place in heaven, sir, to sell the gospel news.

4. I sell the morning paper, sir; my name is Jimmie Brown.
   Everybody knows that I'm the newsboy of the town.
   You can hear me yelling "Morning Star," running along the street.
   Got no hat upon my head, no shoes upon my feet.

Standard Ukulele

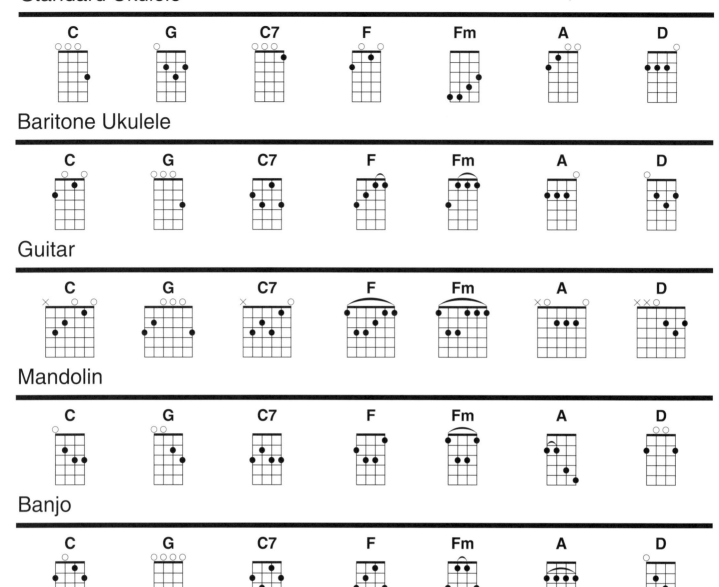

Baritone Ukulele

Guitar

Mandolin

Banjo

Kentucky Waltz

Words and Music by Bill Monroe

Verse
Moderately

We were waltz - ing that night in Ken - tuck - y _____

be - neath the beau - ti - ful har - vest moon,

and I was the boy that was luck - y, _____

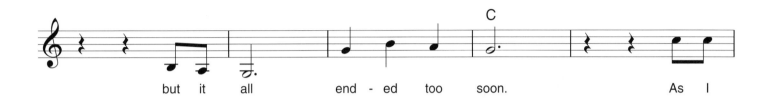

C

but it all end - ed too soon. As I

sit here _____ a - lone _____ in the moon - light, I

C7 F

see your smil - ing face, _____ and I

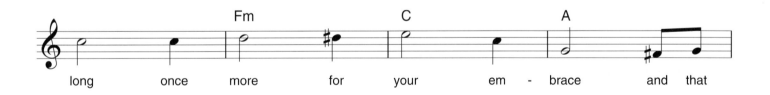

Fm C A

long once more for your em - brace and that

D G C

beau - ti - ful Ken - tuck - y waltz.

Standard Ukulele

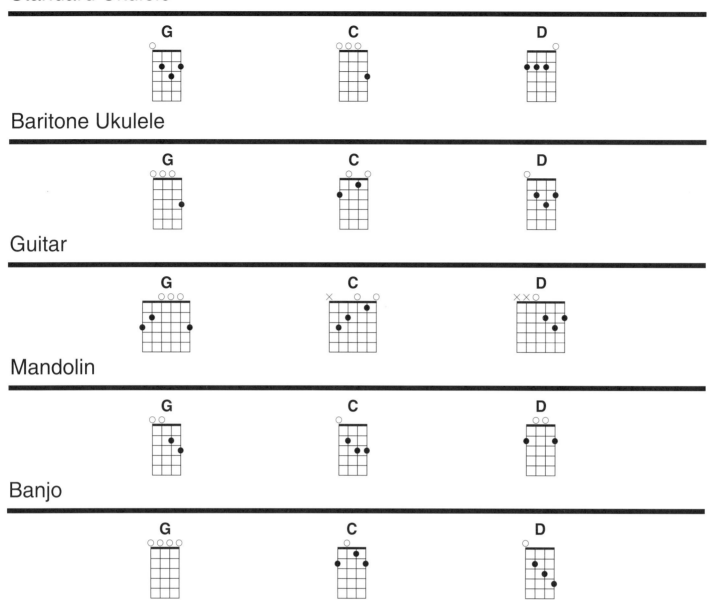

Baritone Ukulele

Guitar

Mandolin

Banjo

Little Cabin Home on the Hill
Words and Music by Lester Flatt and Bill Monroe

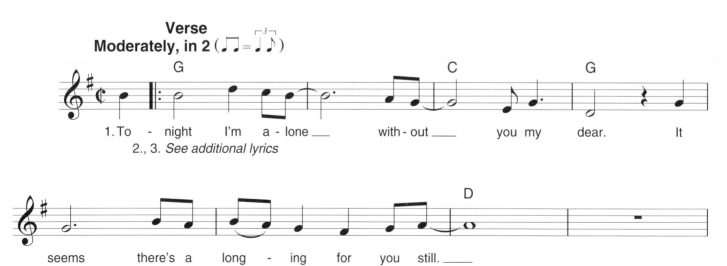

Verse
Moderately, in 2

1. To - night I'm a - lone ___ with - out ___ you my dear. It
2., 3. *See additional lyrics*

seems there's a long - ing for you still. ___

All I have to do _____ now is sit a - lone and cry _____ in our

lit - tle cab - in home on the hill. _____ Oh,

Chorus

some - one has tak - en you from __ me and _ left me

here all __ a - lone. _____ Just lis - ten to the rain _

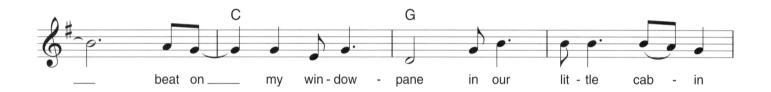

__ beat on _____ my win - dow - pane in our lit - tle cab - in

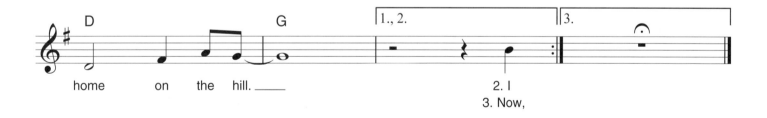

home on the hill. _____

1., 2.

3.

2. I
3. Now,

Additional Lyrics

2. I hope you are happy tonight as you are,
   But in my heart there's a longing for you still.
   I'll just keep it there so I won't be alone
   In our little cabin home on the hill.

3. Now, when you have come to the end of the way
   And find there's no more happiness for you,
   Just let your thoughts turn back once more, if you will,
   To our little cabin home on the hill.

Standard Ukulele

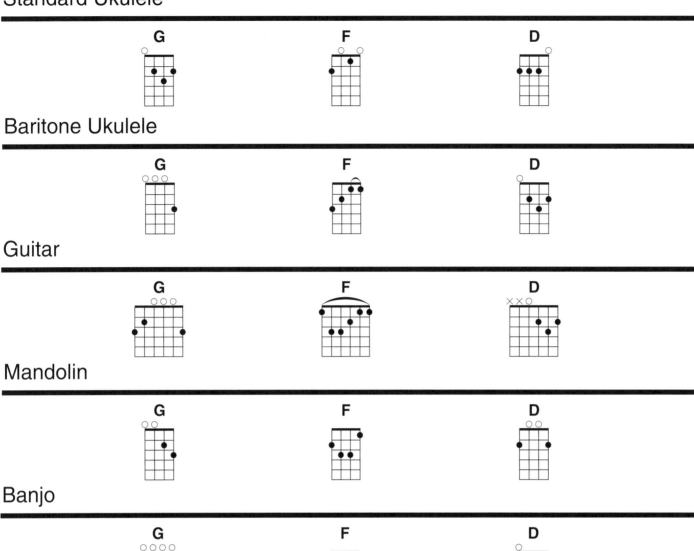

G **F** **D**

Baritone Ukulele

G **F** **D**

Guitar

G **F** **D**

Mandolin

G **F** **D**

Banjo

G **F** **D**

Little Maggie

Traditional

Verse
Moderately fast, in 2

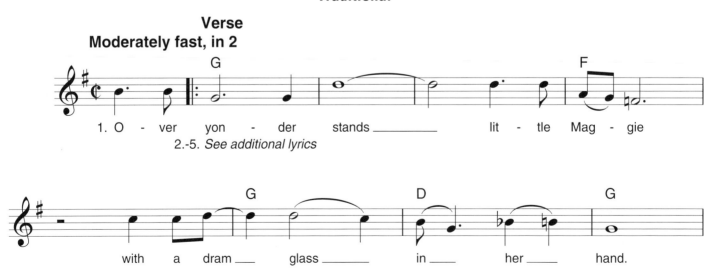

1. O - ver yon - der stands _____ lit - tle Mag - gie
2.-5. *See additional lyrics*

with a dram ___ glass _____ in ___ her ___ hand.

She's   drink - in' a - way _____ her

trou - bles   and   a - court - ing   an - oth - er

man.   2. Pret - ty   3. Last
                        5. Go   a -   4. Lay

Additional Lyrics

2. Pretty flowers were made for bloomin',
   Pretty stars were made to shine.
   Pretty women were made for lovin',
   Little Maggie was made for mine.

3. Last time I saw little Maggie,
   She was sittin' on the banks of the sea
   With a forty-four around her
   And a banjo on her knee.

4. Lay down your last gold dollar,
   Lay down your gold watch and chain.
   Little Maggie's gonna dance for daddy;
   Listen to that old banjo ring.

5. Go away, go away, little Maggie,
   Go and do the best you can.
   I'll get me another woman;
   You can get you another man.

Standard Ukulele

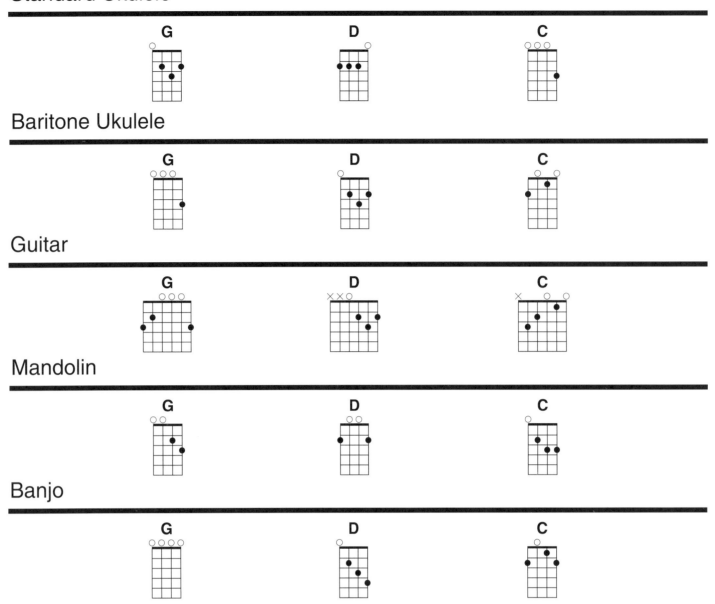

Baritone Ukulele

Guitar

Mandolin

Banjo

The Long Black Veil

Words and Music by Marijohn Wilkin and Danny Dill

Verse
Moderately slow, in 2

1. Ten years a - go, ___ on a cold, ___ dark
2., 3. *See additional lyrics*

night, ___ there was some - one killed 'neath the town ___ hall ___

Additional Lyrics

2. The judge said, "Son what is your alibi?
   If you were somewhere else then you won't have to die."
   I spoke not a word though it meant my life,
   For I had been in the arms of my best friend's wife.

3. The scaffold was high and eternity near.
   She stood in the crowd and shed not a tear.
   And sometimes at night when the cold winds moan,
   In a long black veil she cries o'er my bones.

Standard Ukulele

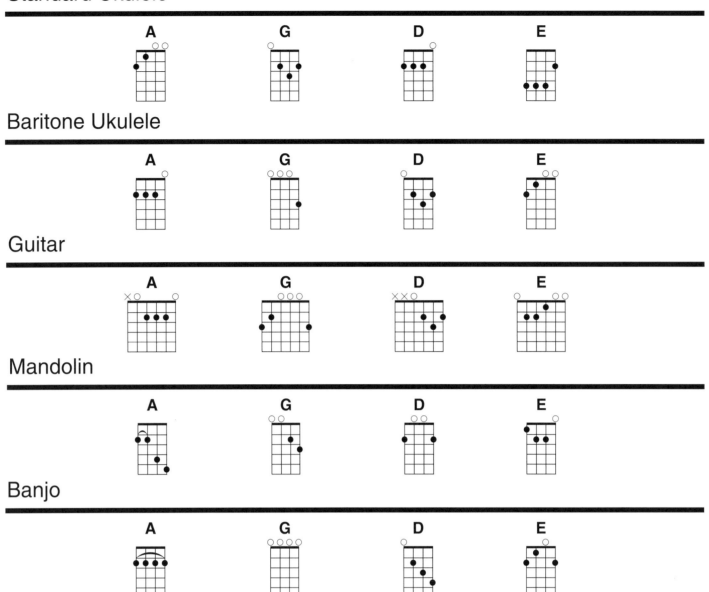

Baritone Ukulele

Guitar

Mandolin

Banjo

Love Please Come Home
Words and Music by Leon Jackson

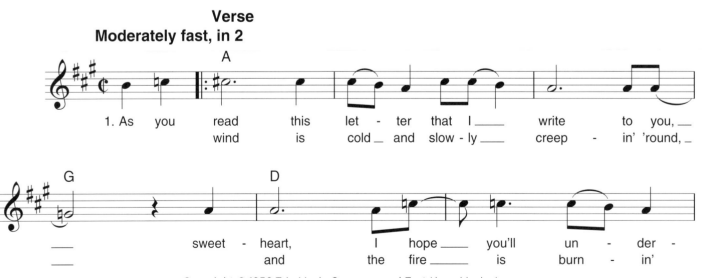

Verse
Moderately fast, in 2

1. As you read this let - ter that I _____ write to you, _____

sweet - heart, I hope _____ you'll un - der -

wind is cold _____ and slow - ly _____ creep - in' 'round, _____

and the fire _____ is burn - in'

stand   that   you're   the   on   -   ly   love __   I
low.   The   snow   has   cov   -   ered   up __   the

knew.   Please   for   -   give __   me   if   you
ground.   Your   ba   -   by's   hun   -   gry,   sick   and

Chorus

can. __ ⎫
cold. __ ⎭   Sweet   -   heart,   I   beg __   you   to   come __

home   to   -   night. _____   I'm   so   blue   and   all __   a   -   lone. __

___   I   prom   -   ise   that   I'll   treat __   you

right.   Love,   oh   love,   oh,   please __   come

home.   2. That   old   home.

Standard Ukulele

Baritone Ukulele

Guitar

Mandolin

Banjo

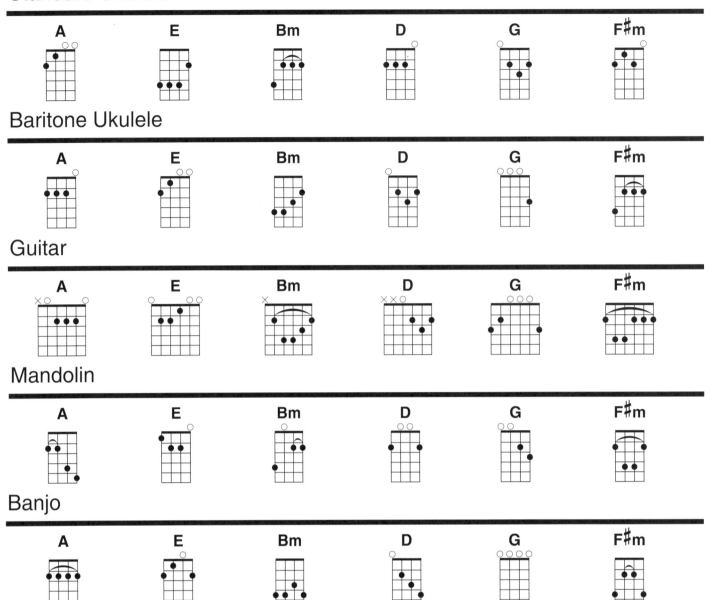

Midnight Moonlight

Words and Music by Peter Rowan

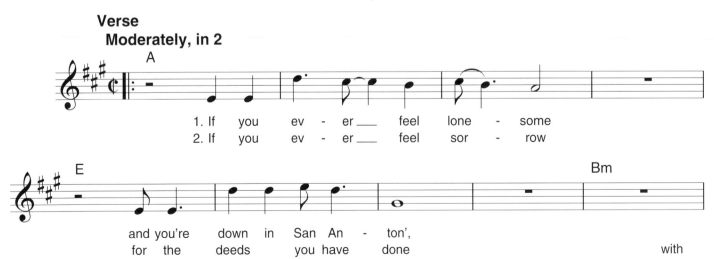

Verse
Moderately, in 2

A

1. If you ev - er ____ feel lone - some
2. If you ev - er ____ feel sor - row

E   Bm

and you're down in San An - ton',
for the deeds you have done   with

Chorus

Standard Ukulele

Baritone Ukulele

Guitar

Mandolin

Banjo

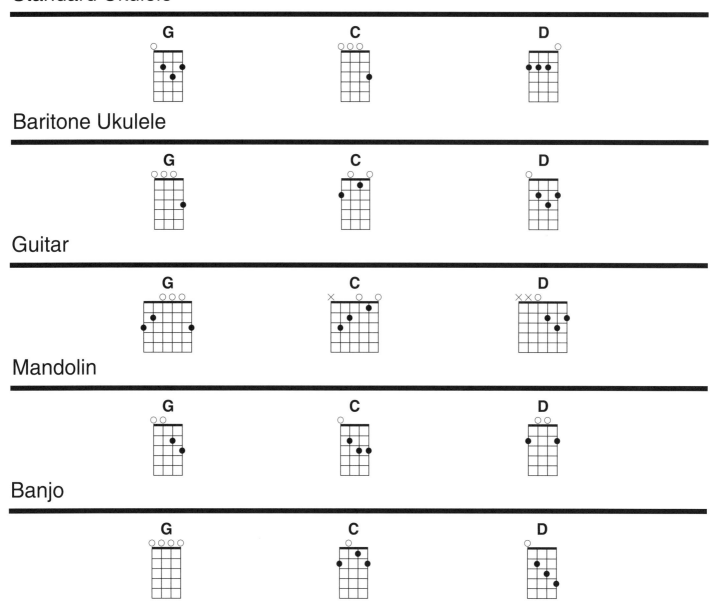

Molly and Tenbrooks
Words and Music by Bill Monroe

Verse
Moderately bright, in 2

1. Run, old Mol - ly run; ____ run old Mol - ly run. ____
3., 5., 7. *See additional lyrics*

Ten-brooks gon - na beat you to the bright shin - in' sun, to the

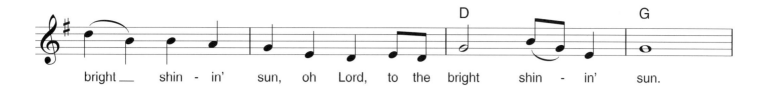

bright __ shin - in' sun, oh Lord, to the bright shin - in' sun.

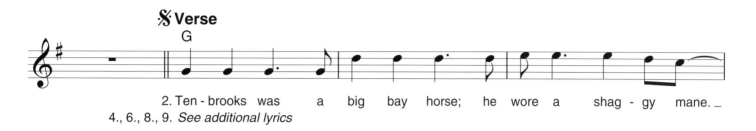

%‌ **Verse**

2. Ten - brooks was a big bay horse; he wore a shag - gy mane. __
4., 6., 8., 9. *See additional lyrics*

__ He run all a - round Mem - phis; he beat the Mem - phis

train, beat the Mem - phis train, oh Lord, beat the Mem - phis

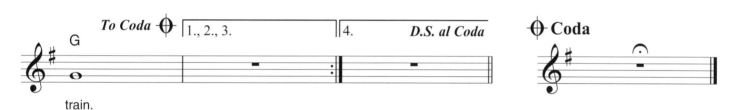

To Coda ⊕ | 1., 2., 3. | | 4. | *D.S. al Coda* ⊕ **Coda**

train.

Additional Lyrics

3. Tenbrooks said to Molly, "What makes your head so red?"
   "Runnin' in the hot sun with a fever in my head,
   Fever in my head, oh Lord, fever in my head."

4. Molly said to Tenbrooks, "You're lookin' mighty squirrel."
   Tenbrooks said to Molly, "I'm leavin' this old world,
   Leavin' this old world, oh Lord, leavin' this old world."

5. Out in California where Molly done as she pleased,
   She came back to old Kentucky, got beat with all ease,
   Beat with all ease, oh Lord, beat with all ease.

6. Women's all a-laughin', children's all a-cryin',
   Men's all a-hollerin', old Tenbrooks is flyin',
   Old Tenbrooks is flyin', oh Lord, old Tenbrooks is flyin'.

7. Kaiper, Kaiper, you're not ridin' right.
   Molly's a-beatin' old Tenbrooks clear out sight,
   Clear out of sight, oh Lord, clear out of sight.

8. Kaiper, Kaiper, Kaiper, my son,
   Give old Tenbrooks the bridle; let old Tenbrooks run,
   Let old Tenbrooks run, oh Lord, let old Tenbrooks run.

9. Go and fetch old Tenbrooks and hitch him in the shade.
   We're gonna bury old Molly in a coffin ready-made,
   Coffin ready-made, oh Lord, coffin ready-made.

Standard Ukulele

Baritone Ukulele

Guitar

Mandolin

Banjo

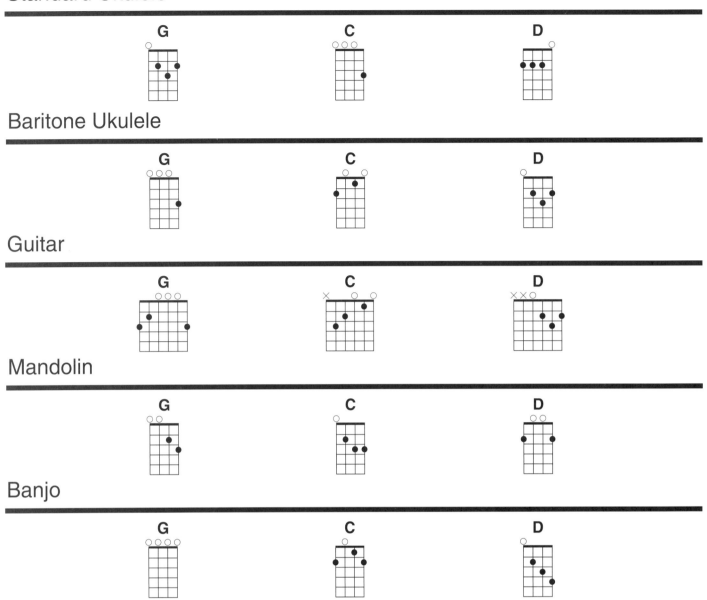

Mountain Dew

Words and Music by Scott Wiseman and Bascom Lunsford

Verse
Moderately fast, in 2

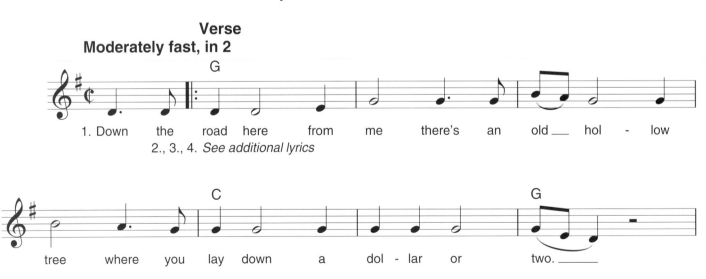

1. Down the road here from me there's an old ___ hol - low
2., 3., 4. *See additional lyrics*

tree where you lay down a dol - lar or two. ___

Go   on a-round   the   bend,   come   back _____ a-

gain,   there's   a   jug   full _____ of that   good old   moun - tain   dew.

Chorus

Oh,   they   call   it   that   good old   moun - tain   dew _____   and

them   that   re - fuse   it   are   few. _____   I'll

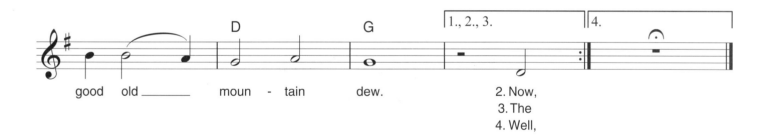

hush   up   my   mug   if   you'll   fill   up _____ my   jug   with   that

good   old _____   moun - tain   dew.   2. Now,
3. The
4. Well,

Additional Lyrics

2. Now, Mr. Roosevelt told 'em just how he felt
   When he heard that the dry law'd gone through.
   If your liquor's too red it'll swell up your head;
   Better stick to that good old mountain dew.

3. The preacher rode by with his head hoisted high,
   Said his wife had been down with the flu.
   He thought that I ort to sell him a quart
   Of my good old mountain dew.

4. Well, my uncle Snort, he's sawed off and short;
   He measures four feet two.
   But he feels like a giant when you give him a pint
   Of that good old mountain dew.

Standard Ukulele

Baritone Ukulele

Guitar

Mandolin

Banjo

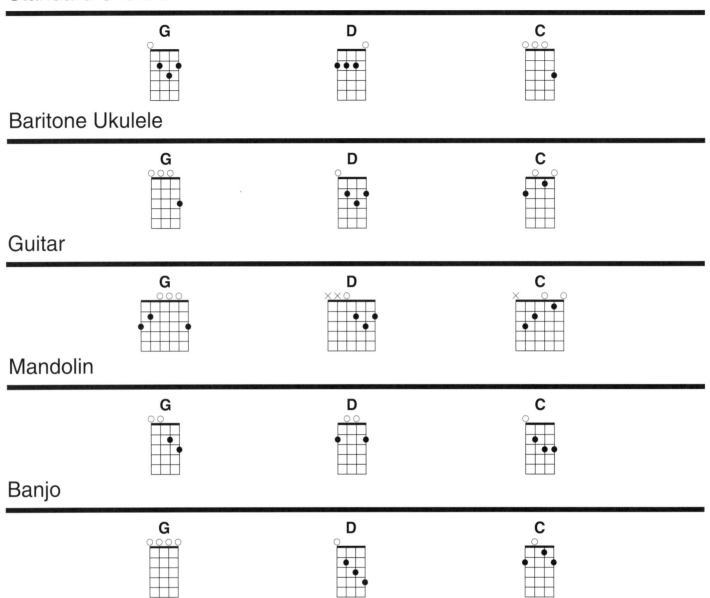

My Walking Shoes

Words and Music by Jimmy Martin and Paul Williams

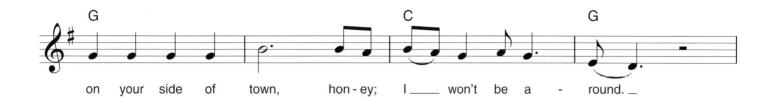

on your side of town, hon-ey; I ___ won't be a - round. __

To Coda ⊕

My walk - ing shoes _ don't fit me an - y - more.

Verse

1. It's a long _____ way from here to o - ver yon - der.
2. I'll be a long _____ time gone from you, ba - by.

My feet, they're get - tin' might - y sore.
You'll nev - er hear me knock up - on your door.

I ain't com - in' back; _ you've made your mind _ to
I thought you were worth _ it once, but I ____ was

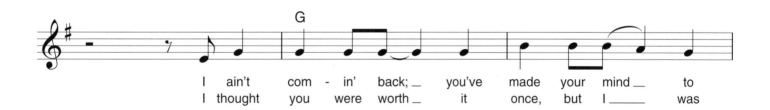

wan - der. ⎫
cra - zy. ⎭   My walk - ing shoes _ don't fit me an - y -

1.   2.   *D.S. al Coda*   ⊕ **Coda**

more. _   My   My

Standard Ukulele

Baritone Ukulele

Guitar

Mandolin

Banjo

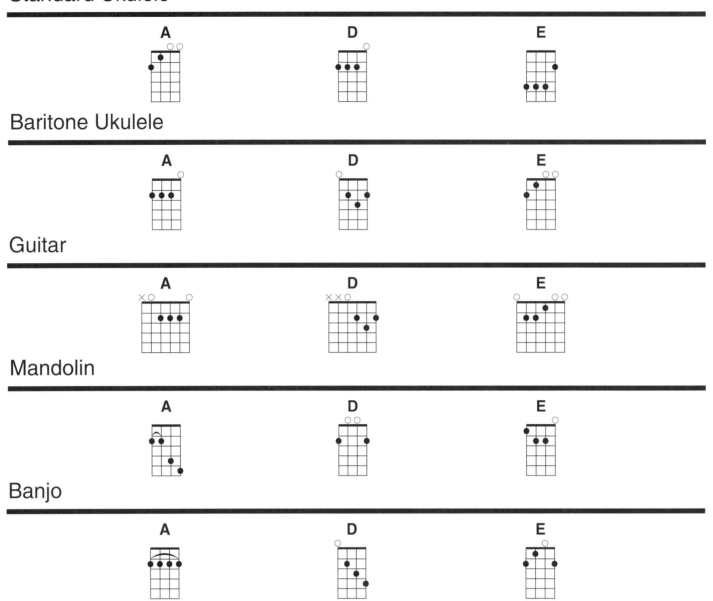

Nine Pound Hammer
Words and Music by Merle Travis

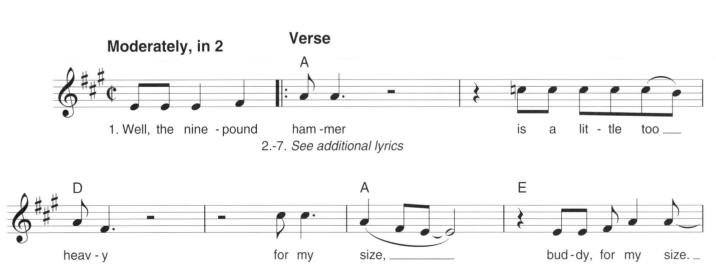

Moderately, in 2

Verse

1. Well, the nine-pound ham-mer is a lit-tle too
2.-7. *See additional lyrics*

heav-y for my size, ___ bud-dy, for my size. ___

Chorus

Roll on, bud - dy; don't you roll __ so

slow. How can I roll _____

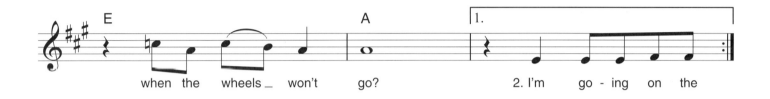

when the wheels __ won't go? 2. I'm go - ing on the

3. Well, there ain't one 4. Rings like 5. It's a long way to

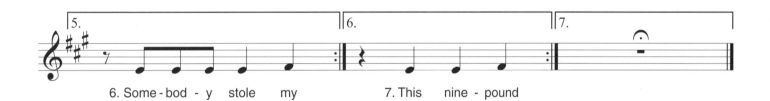

6. Some - bod - y stole my 7. This nine - pound

Additional Lyrics

2. I'm going on the mountain,
   There to see my baby,
   And I ain't comin' back,
   No, I ain't comin' back.

3. Well, there ain't one hammer
   That's in this tunnel
   That'll ring like mine,
   That'll ring like mine.

4. Rings like silver,
   Shines like gold,
   Rings like silver
   And it shines like gold.

5. It's a long way to Harlan
   And a long way to Hazard
   Just to get a little brew,
   Just to get a little brew.

6. Somebody stole
   My nine-pound hammer.
   Lord, they took it and gone.
   Lord, they took it and gone.

7. This nine-pound hammer
   Done killed John Henry.
   Ain't gonna kill me,
   Ain't gonna kill me.

Standard Ukulele

| G | B7 | C | D | A7 |

Baritone Ukulele

| G | B7 | C | D | A7 |

Guitar

| G | B7 | C | D | A7 |

Mandolin

| G | B7 4fr | C | D | A7 |

Banjo

| G | B7 | C | D | A7 |

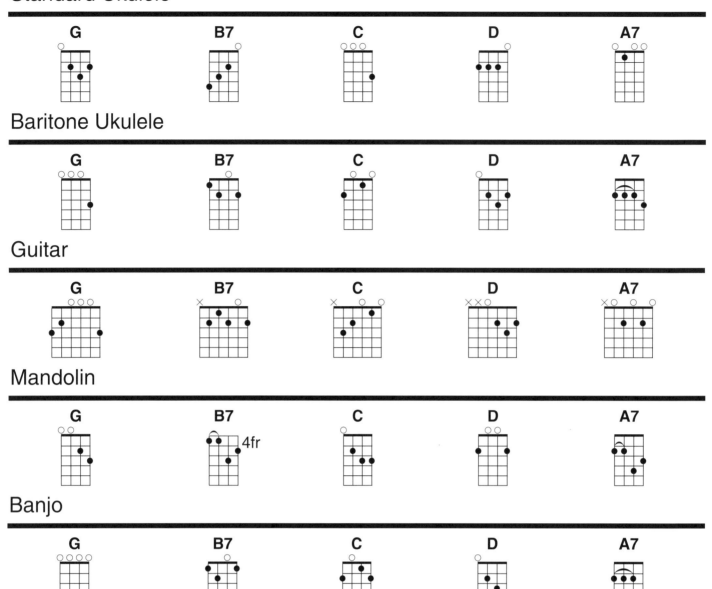

Old Home Place

Words by Mitch Jayne
Music by Dean Webb

% Verse

Moderately, in 2

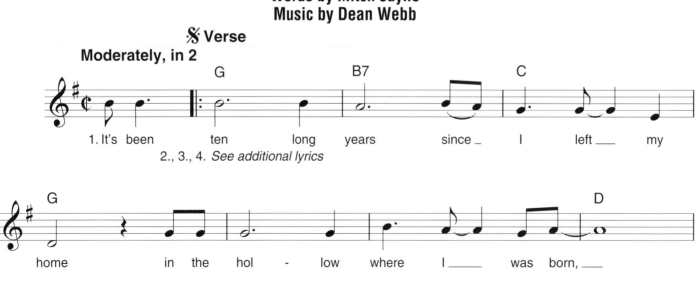

1. It's been ten long years since ___ I left ___ my

2., 3., 4. *See additional lyrics*

home in the hol - low where I ___ was born, ___

Additional Lyrics

2. I fell in love with a girl in the town;
   I thought that she would be true.
   I ran away to Charlottesville
   And worked in a sawmill crew.

3. The girl ran off with somebody else;
   The tariffs took my pay.
   And now I stand where the old home stood
   Before they took it away.

4. Now the geese fly south and the wind grows cold
   As I stand here and hang my head.
   I've lost my love. I've lost my home.
   And now I wish that I was dead.

91

Standard Ukulele

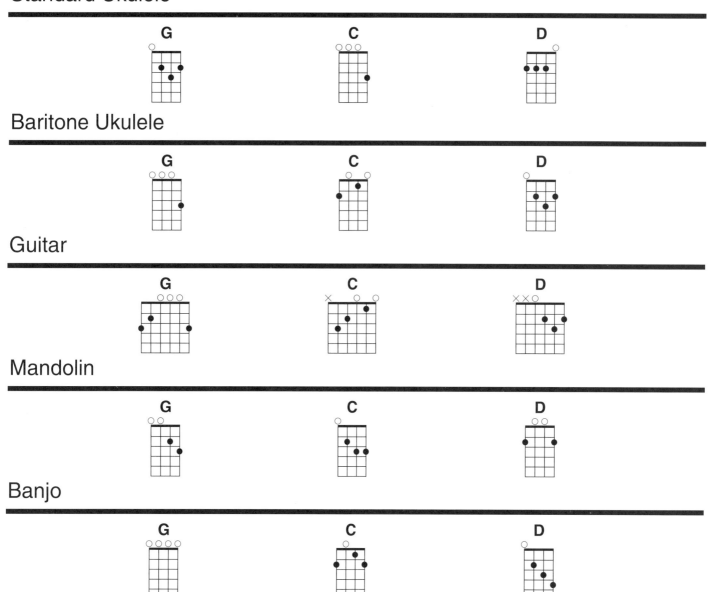

Baritone Ukulele

Guitar

Mandolin

Banjo

On & On
Words and Music by Bill Monroe

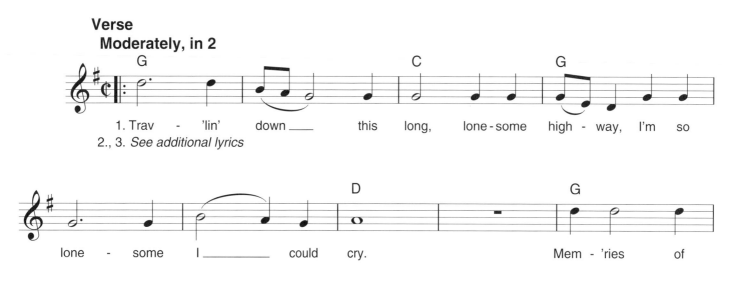

Verse
Moderately, in 2

1. Trav - 'lin' down ____ this long, lone - some high - way, I'm so
2., 3. *See additional lyrics*

lone - some I ____ could cry. Mem - 'ries of

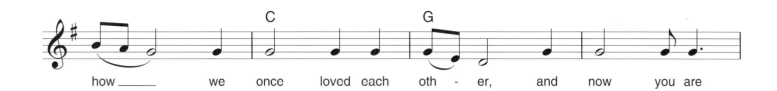

how _____ we once loved each oth - er, and now you are

say - ing ___ good - bye.   On and

on _____ I fol - low my dar - lin', and I won - der

where she ___ can be.   On and

on _____ I fol - low my dar - lin', and I won - der if she

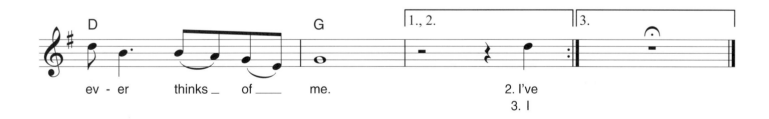

ev - er thinks _ of ___ me.   2. I've
                                                3. I

Additional Lyrics

2. I've cried, I've cried, for you, little darlin';
   It breaks my heart to hear your name.
   My friends, they all so love you, my darling,
   And they think that I am to blame.

3. I have to follow you, my darling;
   I can't sleep when the sun goes down.
   By your side is my destination;
   The road is clear and that's where I'm bound.

Standard Ukulele

Baritone Ukulele

Guitar

Mandolin

Banjo

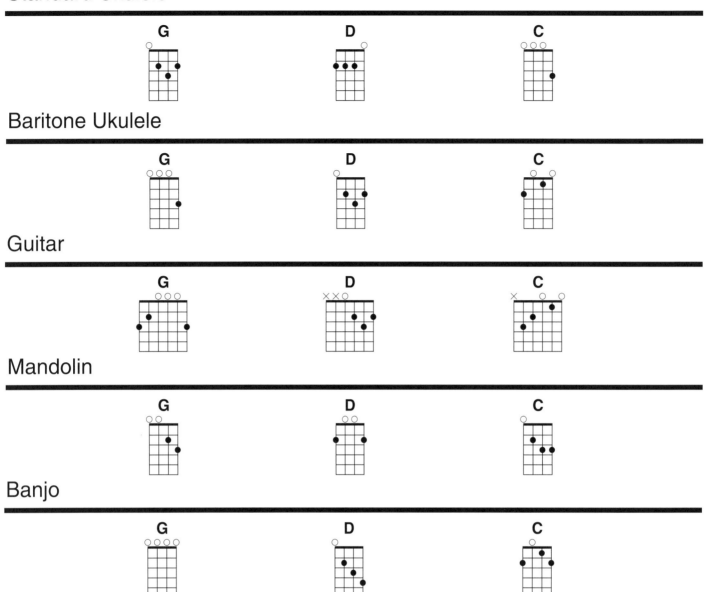

Once More
Words and Music by Robert Owens

Moderately

𝄋 Chorus

G

Once more _____ to be ___ with you, ___ dear,

D

just for to - night, ___ to hold ___ you tight. ___

Once   more _____ I'd   give   a   for   -   tune

if   I _____ could   see _____ you   once ____

Verse

Fine

more.   For   -   get   the   past; __   this

hurt   can't   last.   Oh.   I _____ don't   want __   it   to

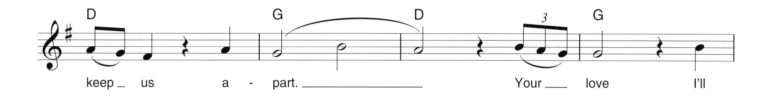

keep __   us   a   -   part. _____   Your __   love   I'll

crave; __   I'll   be   your   slave   if   you'll ___   just

D.S. al Fine

give __   me   all ___   of   your   heart.   Once

Standard Ukulele

Baritone Ukulele

Guitar

Mandolin

Banjo

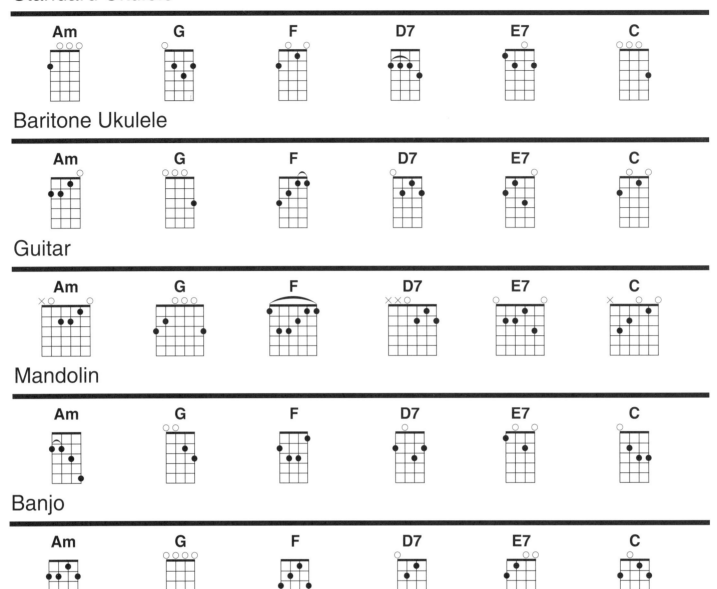

Panama Red
Words and Music by Peter Rowan

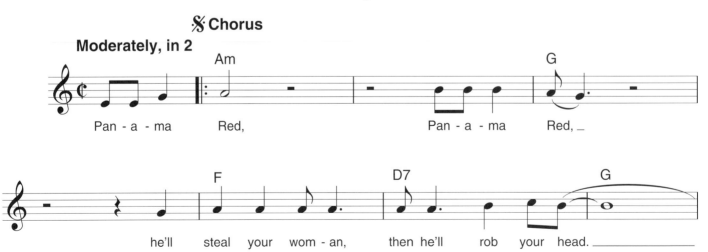

Moderately, in 2

𝄋 Chorus

Pan - a - ma Red, Pan - a - ma Red, __

he'll steal your wom - an, then he'll rob your head. ____

Standard Ukulele

Baritone Ukulele

Guitar

Mandolin

Banjo

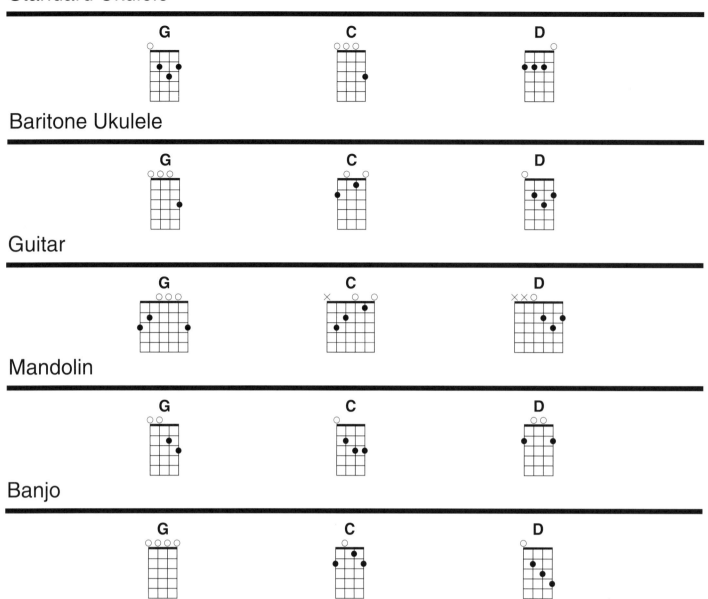

Pig in the Pen

Words and Music by Ralph Stanley and Carter Stanley

Chorus
Moderately fast, in 2

G

I got a pig home in a pen, corn to feed him

C   G

on.   All I need is a pret-ty lit-tle girl to

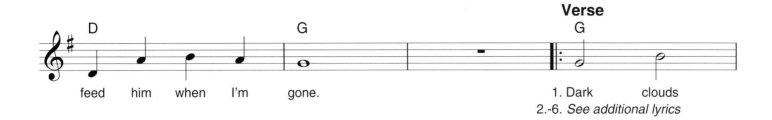

feed   him   when   I'm   gone.

Verse

1. Dark   clouds
2.-6. *See additional lyrics*

roll - ing   in,   sure   sign   of   rain.   Get   the   old   blue

bon - net   on,   sweet   lit - tle   Li - za   Jane.

Chorus

I   got   a   pig   home   in   a   pen,

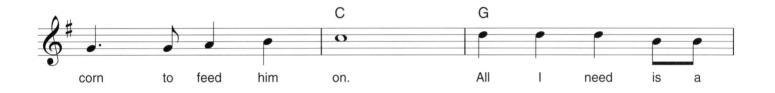

corn   to   feed   him   on.   All   I   need   is   a

Play 6 times

pret - ty   lit - tle   girl   to   feed   him   when   I'm   gone.

Additional Lyrics

2. Goin' on the mountain to sow a little cane.
   Raise a barrel of sorghum to sweet lil' Liza Jane.

3. Yonder comes that gal of mine; how you think I know?
   I can tell by that gingham gown hangin' down so low.

4. Bake them biscuits, baby; bake 'em good 'n' brown.
   When you get them biscuits baked we're Alabamy bound.

5. When she sees me comin', she wrings her hands and cries,
   Says, "Yonder comes the sweetest boy that ever lived or died."

6. Now, when she sees me leavin', she wrings her hands and cries,
   "Yonder goes the meanest boy that ever lived or died."

Standard Ukulele

Baritone Ukulele

Guitar

Mandolin

Banjo

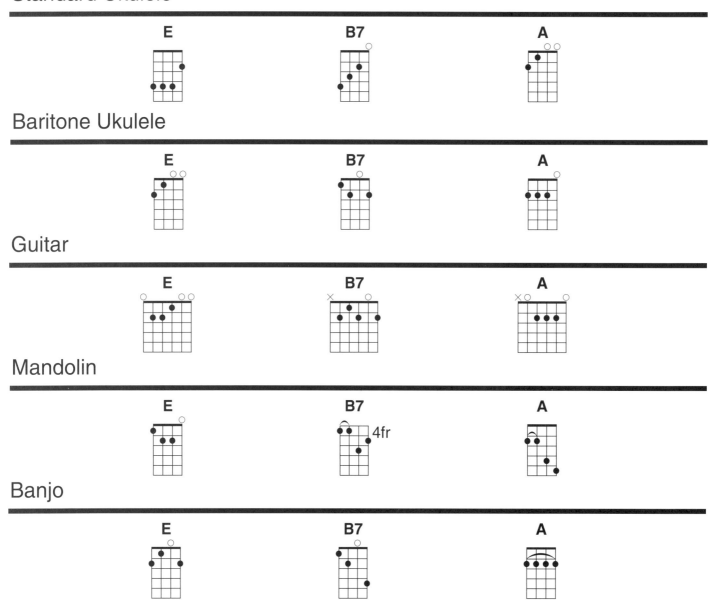

Rank Strangers to Me

Words and Music by Albert E. Brumley

Slowly, in 4

Verse

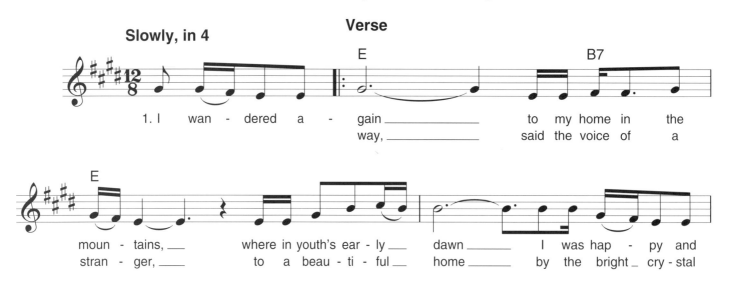

1. I wan - dered a - gain to my home in the
way, said the voice of a

moun - tains, where in youth's ear - ly dawn I was hap - py and
stran - ger, to a beau - ti - ful home by the bright cry - stal

frcc. I looked _ for my friends, _____ but I nev - er could
sea. Some beau - ti - ful day _____ I'll meet them in

find _ them. ___ I found they were _ all _____ rank stran - gers to _
heav - en, _____ where no one will _ be _____ a stran - ger to _

Chorus

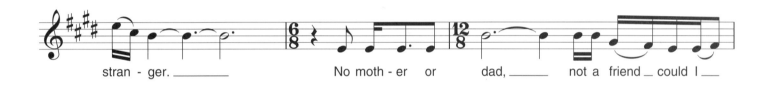

me. }
me. } Ev -'ry - bod - y I met _____ seemed to be a rank

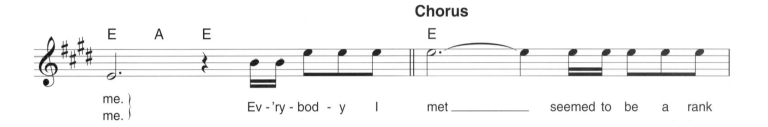

stran - ger. _____ No moth - er or dad, _____ not a friend _ could I _

see. They knew _ not my name _____ and I knew not their

fac - es. _____ I found they were _ all _____ rank stran - gers to

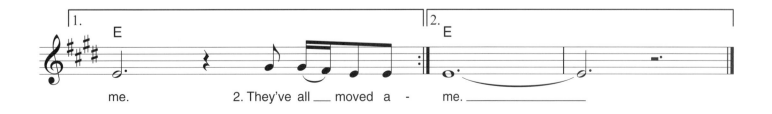

me. 2. They've all _ moved a - me. _____

Standard Ukulele

Baritone Ukulele

Guitar

Mandolin

Banjo

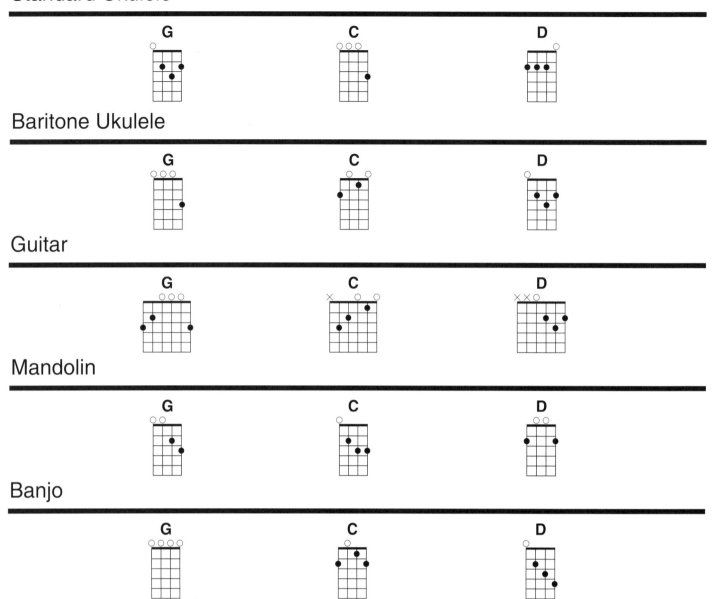

Ridin' That Midnight Train

Words and Music by Carter Stanley

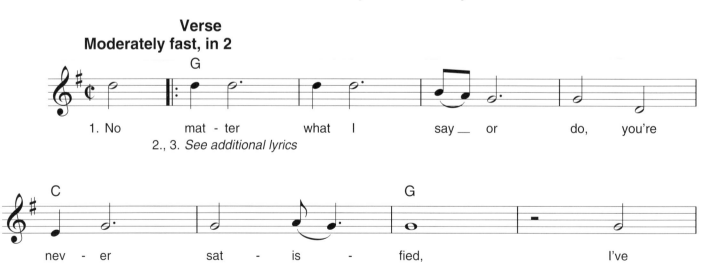

Verse
Moderately fast, in 2

G

1. No mat - ter what I say ___ or do, you're
2., 3. *See additional lyrics*

C   G

nev - er sat - is - fied,   I've

tried and tried so man - y times. _____ I'm

D ... **G**

leav - in' you now; good - bye. I'm

Chorus

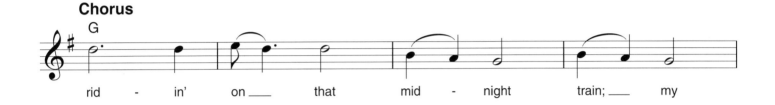

G

rid - in' on _____ that mid - night train; _____ my

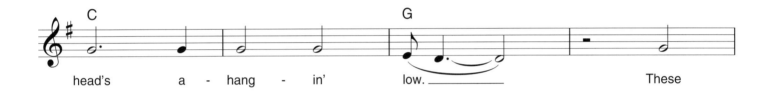

C ... **G**

head's a - hang - in' low. _____ These

aw - ful blues will fol - low me _____ wher -

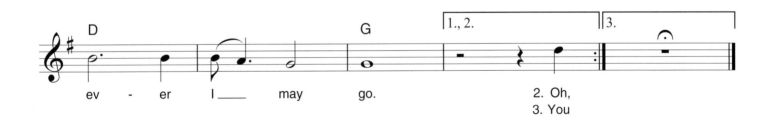

D ... **G** ... 1., 2. ... 3.

ev - er I _____ may go. 2. Oh,
3. You

Additional Lyrics

2. Oh, why on earth was I ever born?
   I'll never understand.
   To fall in love with a woman like you,
   In love with another man.

3. You broke a heart that trusted you.
   Why wasn't it made of stone?
   I'm left in a world black as night,
   Yet I must travel alone.

Standard Ukulele

Baritone Ukulele

Guitar

Mandolin

Banjo

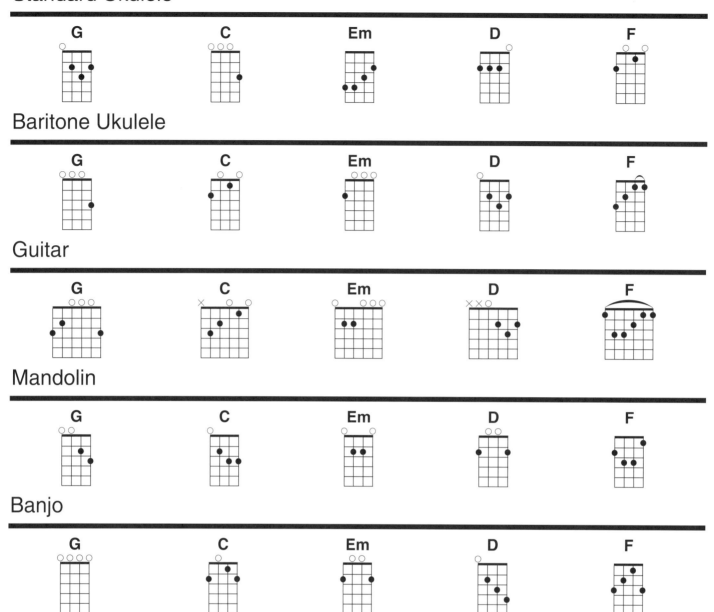

Rocky Top
Words and Music by Boudleaux Bryant and Felice Bryant

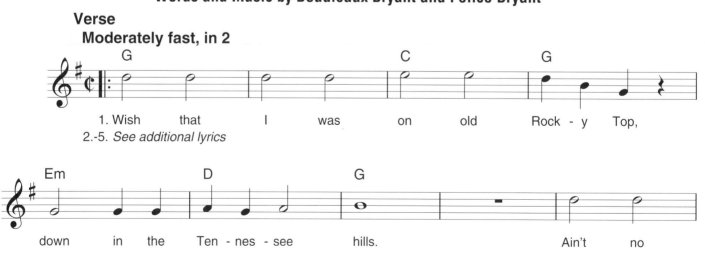

Verse
Moderately fast, in 2

1. Wish that I was on old Rock - y Top,
2.-5. *See additional lyrics*

down in the Ten - nes - see hills. Ain't no

Additional Lyrics

2. Once I had a girl on Rocky Top,
   Half bear, the other half cat.
   Wild as a mink, but sweet as soda pop;
   I still dream about that.

3. Once two strangers climbed old Rocky Top
   Looking for a moonshine still.
   Strangers ain't come down from Rocky Top;
   Reckon they never will.

4. Corn won't grow at all on Rocky Top;
   Dirt's too rocky by far.
   That's why all the folks on Rocky Top
   Get their corn from a jar.

5. I've had years of cramped-up city life,
   Trapped like a duck in a pen.
   All I know is it's a pity
   Life can't be simple again.

Standard Ukulele

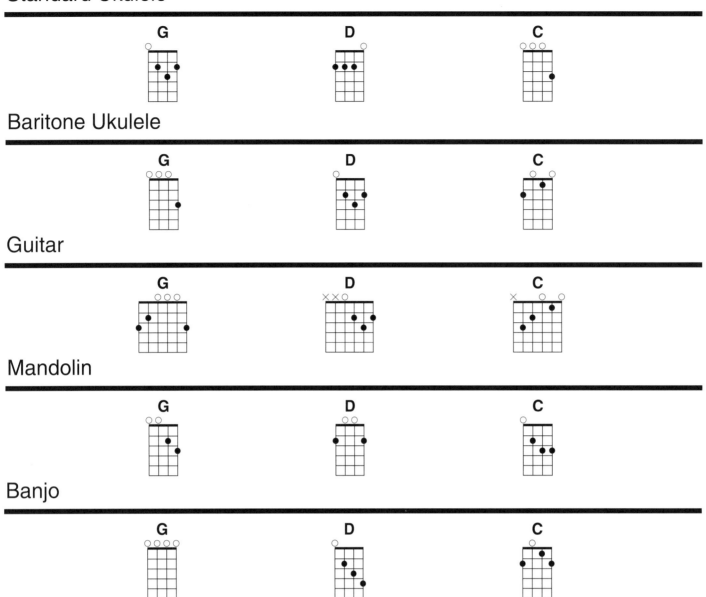

Baritone Ukulele

Guitar

Mandolin

Banjo

Roll in My Sweet Baby's Arms
Traditional

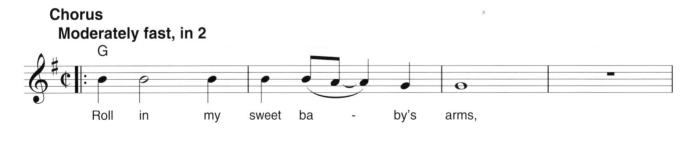

Chorus
Moderately fast, in 2

Roll in my sweet ba - by's arms,

roll in my sweet ba - by's arms.

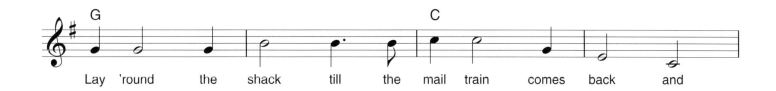

Lay 'round the shack till the mail train comes back and

roll in my sweet ba - by's arms. *Fine* 1. I

Verse

ain't gon - na work on _____ no rail - road,
2., 3. *See additional lyrics*

ain't gon - na work on no farm. _____

Lay 'round the shack till the mail train comes back and

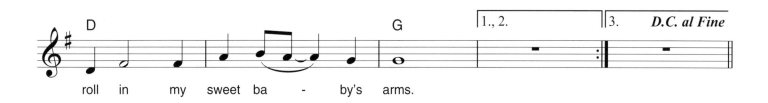

roll in my sweet ba - by's arms.

Additional Lyrics

2. Now, where was you last Friday night
While I was lyin' in jail?
Walkin' the streets with another man;
Wouldn't even go my bail.

3. I know your parents don't like me;
They drove me away from your door.
Had my life to live over,
I'd never go there anymore.

Standard Ukulele

Baritone Ukulele

Guitar

Mandolin

Banjo

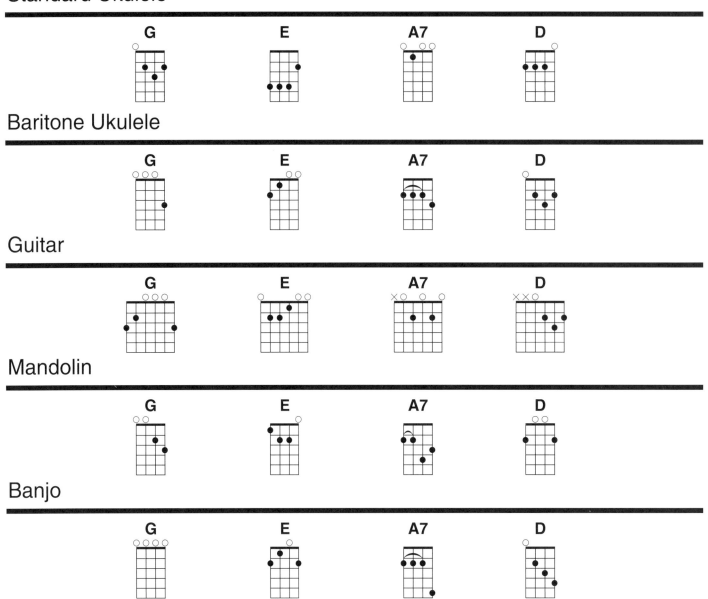

Salty Dog Blues

Words and Music by Wiley A. Morris and Zeke Morris

Verse
Moderately fast, in 2

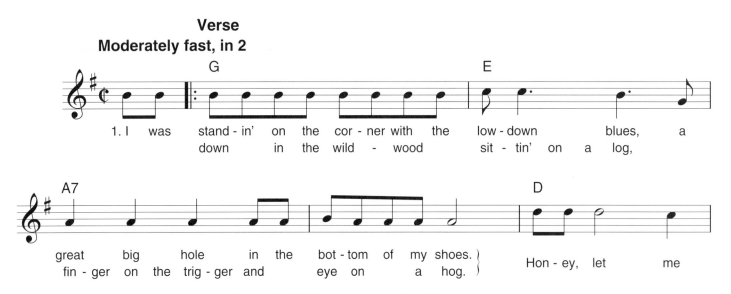

1. I was stand - in' on the cor - ner with the low - down blues, a
down in the wild - wood sit - tin' on a log,

great big hole in the bot - tom of my shoes.
fin - ger on the trig - ger and eye on a hog.

Hon - ey, let me

Standard Ukulele

Baritone Ukulele

Guitar

Mandolin

Banjo

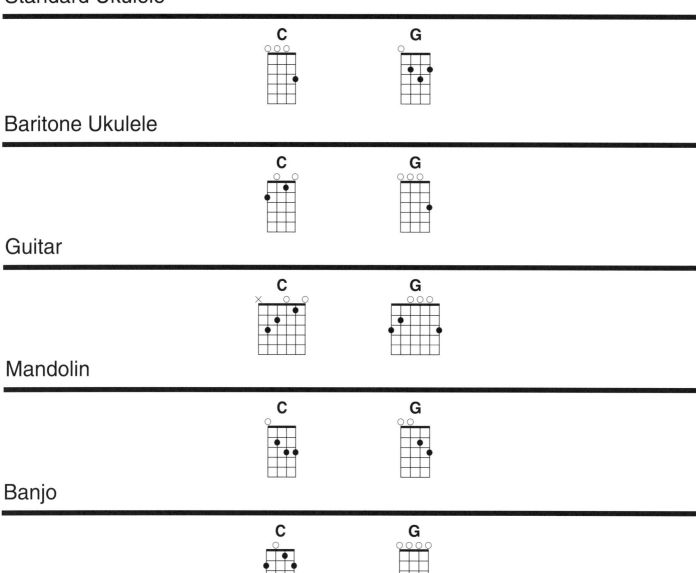

Shady Grove

Appalachian Folk Song

Verse
Fast, in 2

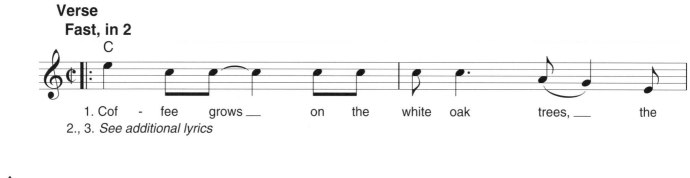

1. Cof - fee grows __ on the white oak trees, __ the
2., 3. *See additional lyrics*

riv - er flows with bran - dy. The rocks on the hill all

cov - ered with gold ___ and the girls all sweet - er than can - dy.

Chorus

Shad - y grove, ___ my _____ lit - tle miss; ___ shad - y grove ___ my

dar - lin'. Shad - y grove, ___ my _____ lit - tle miss; ___

go - in' back to Har - lan. 2. Well, I Har - lan. Har - lan.

Additional Lyrics

2. Well, I guess you think, my pretty little miss,
   I can't live without you.
   I'll let you know, before I go,
   I care a little about you.

3. Every time I go that road,
   It's always dark and cloudy.
   Every time I see that gal,
   I always tell her howdy.

Standard Ukulele

Baritone Ukulele

Guitar

Mandolin

Banjo

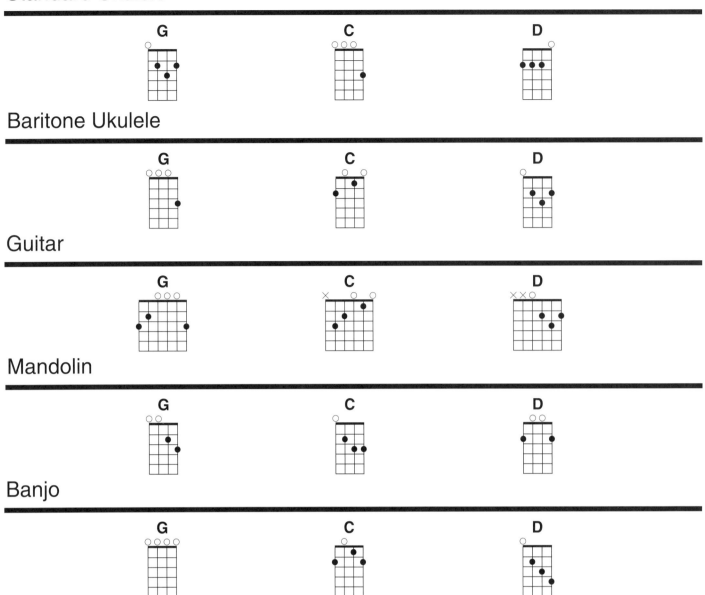

Sitting on Top of the World

Words and Music by Walter Jacobs and Lonnie Carter

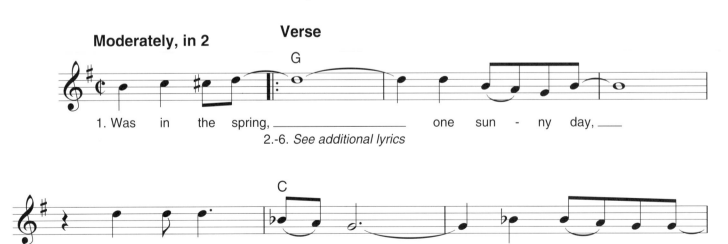

Moderately, in 2

Verse

1. Was in the spring, _____ one sun - ny day, _____

2.-6. *See additional lyrics*

my good gal left ___ me; ___ she went ___ a - way. ___

Now she's gone _____ and I don't

wor - ry. Lord, I'm sit - ting on top _____ of __ the world. __

|1.–5. |6.|

— 2. She called me up __
3. Ash - es to ash -
4. Mis - sis - sip - pi Riv -
5. If you don't like my peach -
6. Don't come to me __

Additional Lyrics

2. She called me up from down in El Paso,
   Said, "Come home, Daddy; I need you so."
   Now she's gone and I don't worry.
   Lord, I'm sitting on top of the world.

3. Ashes to ashes and dust to dust;
   Show me a woman that a man can trust.
   Now she's gone and I don't worry.
   Lord, I'm sitting on top of the world.

4. Mississippi River runs deep and wide.
   The gal I'm loving is on the other side.
   Now she's gone and I don't worry.
   Lord, I'm sitting on top of the world.

5. If you don't like my peaches, don't you shake my tree.
   Stay out of my orchard and let the peaches be.
   Now she's gone and I don't worry.
   Lord, I'm sitting on top of the world.

6. Don't come to me holding out your hand.
   I'll get me a woman just like you got your man.
   Now she's gone and I don't worry.
   Lord, I'm sitting on top of the world.

Standard Ukulele

Baritone Ukulele

Guitar

Mandolin

Banjo

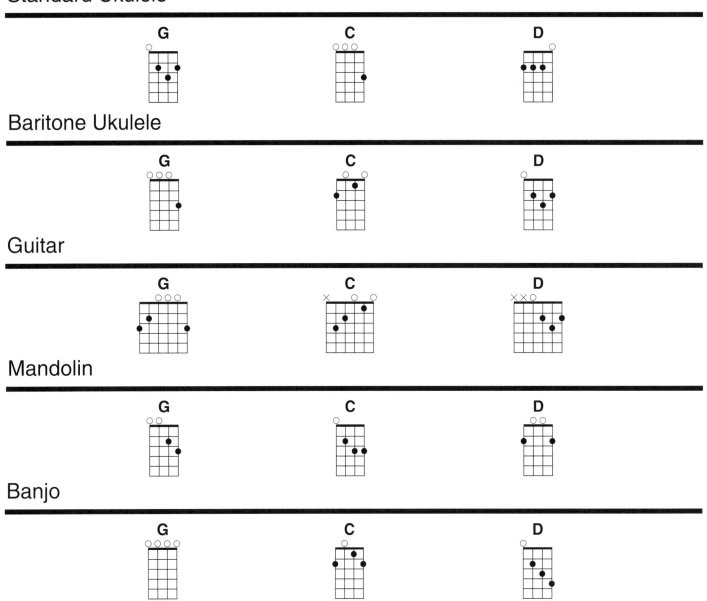

Sophronie

Words and Music by Alton Delmore and D.C. Mullins

Chorus
Moderately, in 2

G   C

Love 'em   and   leave ____ 'em,   kiss 'em and

D   G

grieve ___ 'em.   That used   to   be   my   mot - to   so

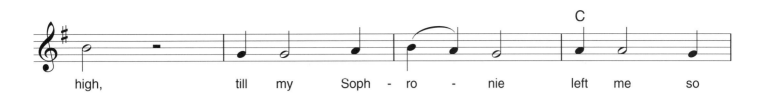

high, till my Soph - ro - nie left me so

lone - ly, and now there's a tear - drop in my eye.

Verse

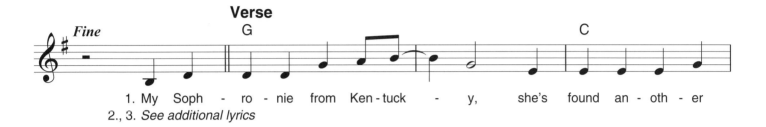

1. My Soph - ro - nie from Ken - tuck - y, she's found an - oth - er
2., 3. *See additional lyrics*

man. I can't e - ven kiss her, can't e - ven hold __ her

hand. _____ The moon we used __ to love ___ be - neath __ is

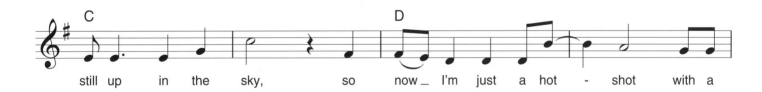

still up in the sky, so now __ I'm just a hot - shot with a

tear - drop in my eye. _____

Additional Lyrics

2. Till Gabriel blows his bugle, I'll be lovin' that sweet girl.
   She means more to me than the whole wide world.
   I used to be a killer with the women, me oh my,
   But now I'm just a hotshot with a teardrop in my eye.

3. I used to slay the pretty girls from Maine to Alabam'.
   I love them very much at first, then I let them down.
   I've seen so many pretty eyes been filled with bitter tears,
   Find them and forget them, but now I have my fears.

Standard Ukulele

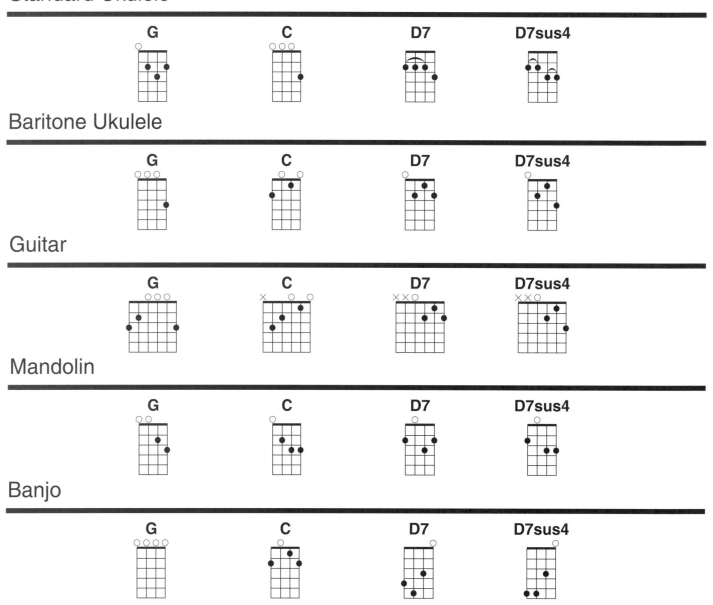

Baritone Ukulele

Guitar

Mandolin

Banjo

Turn Your Radio On
Words and Music by Albert E. Brumley

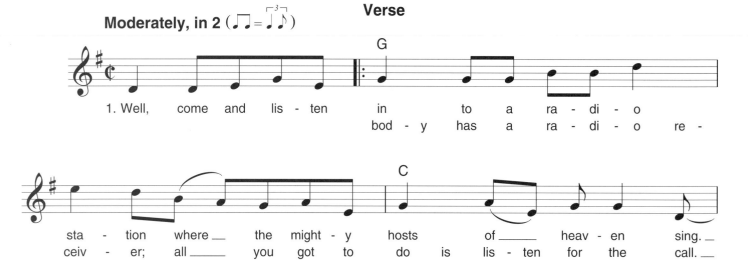

1. Well, come and lis-ten in to a ra-di-o sta-tion where __ the might-y hosts of __ heav-en sing.

bod-y has a ra-di-o re-ceiv-er; all __ you got to do is lis-ten for the call. __

Standard Ukulele

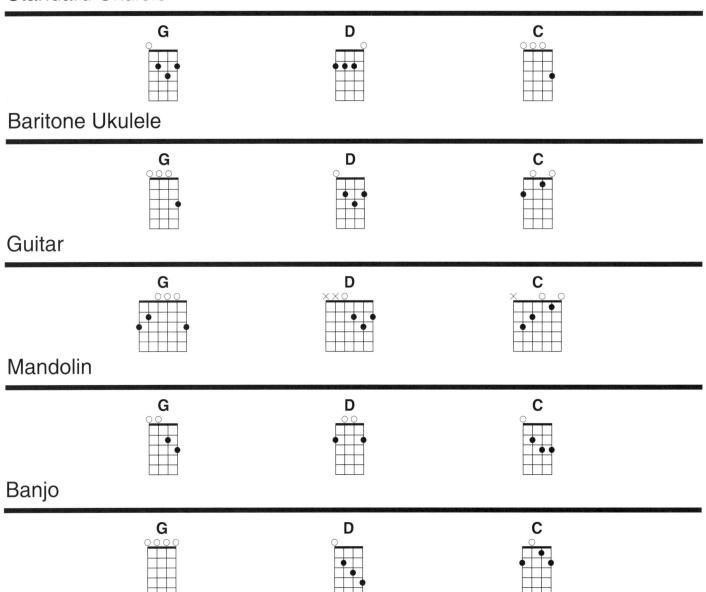

Baritone Ukulele

Guitar

Mandolin

Banjo

Uncle Pen
Words and Music by Bill Monroe

Moderately, in 2   **Verse**

G

1. Oh, the peo - ple would come from far a - way;___ they
2., 3. *See additional lyrics*

danced all___ night till the break of day. When the call - er would hol - er,

"Do - si - do," __ you knew Un - cle Pen was read - y to go. _____

Chorus

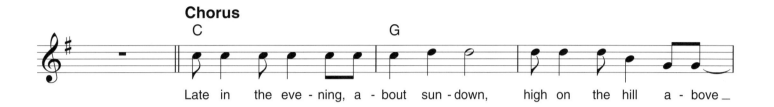

Late in the eve - ning, a - bout sun - down, high on the hill a - bove __

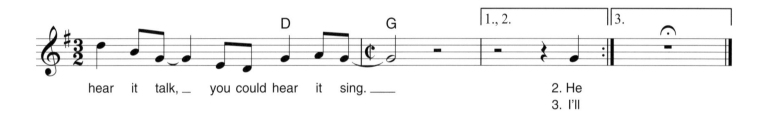

__ the town, __ Un - cle Pen played the fid - dle; Lord, how it would ring! __ You could

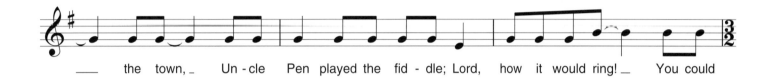

hear it talk, __ you could hear it sing. ____

1., 2.   3.

2. He
3. I'll

Additional Lyrics

2. He played an old piece called "Soldier's Joy"
   And the one called "Boston Boy."
   The greatest of all was "Jenny Lynn";
   To me that's where it'd really begin.

3. I'll never forget that mournful day
   When Uncle Pen was called away.
   He hung up his fiddle, he hung up his bow;
   We knew it was time for him to go.

Standard Ukulele

Baritone Ukulele

Guitar

Mandolin

Banjo

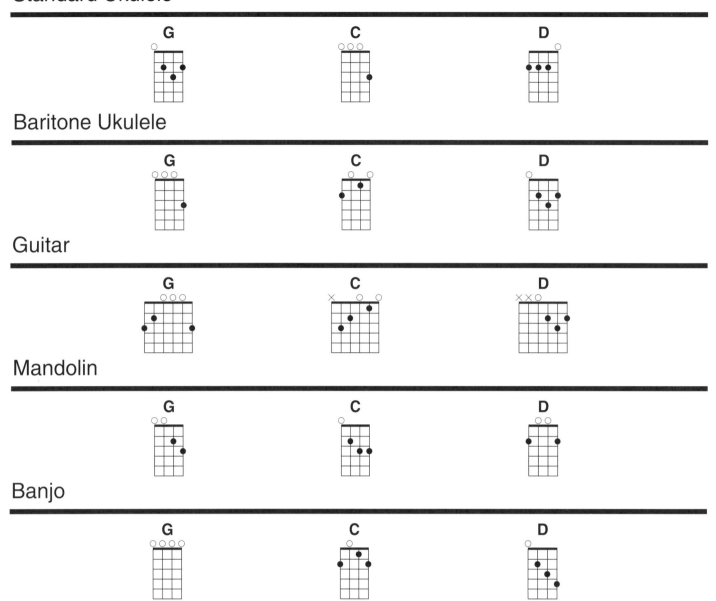

Wabash Cannonball
Words and Music by A.P. Carter

Verse
Moderately, in 2

1. From the great At - lan - tic O - cean to the wide Pa - cif - ic
2., 3., 4. *See additional lyrics*

shore, from the queen of flow - ing moun - tains to the south _ bells by _ the

Chorus

shore. She's might-y tall and hand - some and __ known quite well by

all. She's the com-bi-na - tion of the Wa-bash Can-non -

ball. Oh, lis-ten to the jin-gle, ____ the

rum-ble and __ the roar as she glides a-long the wood-lands to the

hills __ and by __ the shore. ___ Hear the might-y rush __ of the en-gine, hear the

lone-some ho-bo's call. You're trav-'ling through the jun-gle on the

Wa-bash Can-non - ball. 2. The

Additional Lyrics

2. The Eastern states are dandy, so all the people say,
   From New York to Saint Louis and Chicago by the way.
   From the hills of Minnesota, where the rippling waters fall,
   No chances can be taken on the Wabash Cannonball.

3. She came down from Birmingham one cold December day,
   As she rolled into the station, you could hear all the people say.
   There's a gal from Tennessee; she's long and she's tall.
   She came down from Birmingham on the Wabash Cannonball.

4. Here's to Daddy Claxton; may his name forever stand
   And always be remembered 'round the courts of Alabam'.
   His earthly race is over and the curtains 'round him fall.
   We'll carry him home to victory on the Wabash Cannonball.

Standard Ukulele

Baritone Ukulele

Guitar

Mandolin

Banjo

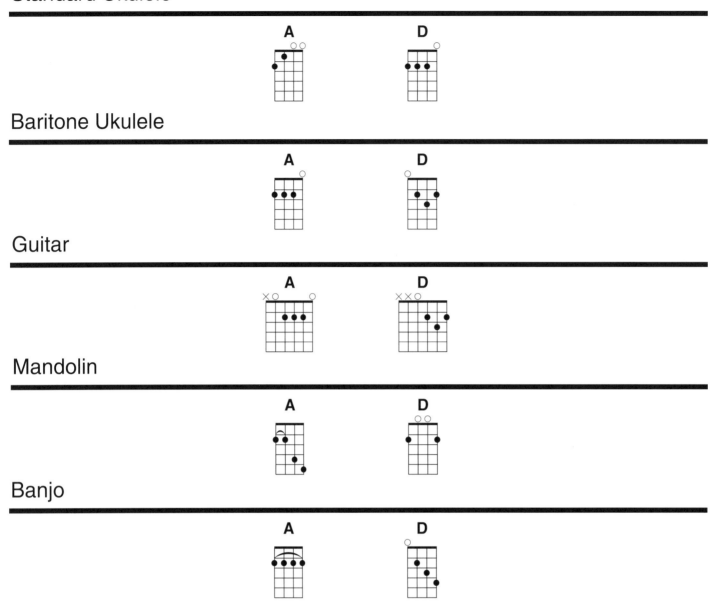

Walls of Time
Words and Music by Bill Monroe

Verse
Moderately slow, in 2

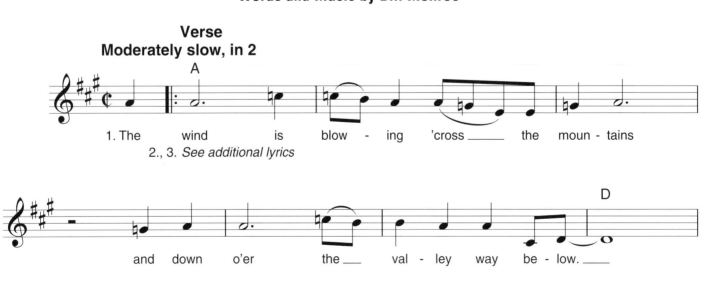

1. The wind is blow - ing 'cross ___ the moun - tains
2., 3. *See additional lyrics*

and down o'er the ___ val - ley way be - low. ___

It sweeps the grave ___ of ___ my dar - ling;

when I die, _____ that's where I want ___ to go. ___

Chorus

Lord, send the an - gels for ___ my dar - lin'

and take _____ her ___ to that home on high. I'll

wait my time ___ out here ___ on earth, ___ love, and

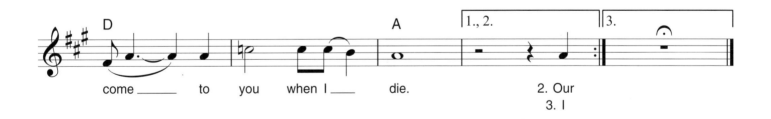

come _____ to you when I ___ die. 2. Our
3. I

Additional Lyrics

2. Our names are carved upon the tombstones;
   I promised you before you died.
   Our love will bloom forever, darling,
   When we rest side by side.

3. I hear a voice out in the darkness;
   It moans and whispers through the pines.
   I know it's my sweetheart a-calling;
   I hear her through the walls of time.

Standard Ukulele

Baritone Ukulele

Guitar

Mandolin

Banjo

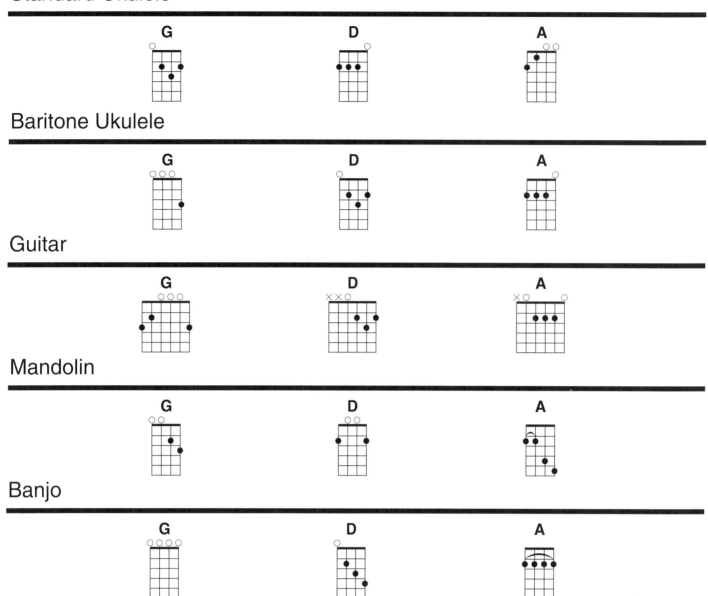

Way Down Town

Traditional

Chorus
Moderately fast, in 2

Way down - town, just a - fool - in' a - round,

took me to the ___ jail. It's

oh   me,   and   it's   oh _____   my,

no   one   to   go   my ___   bail.   1. It   was

Verse

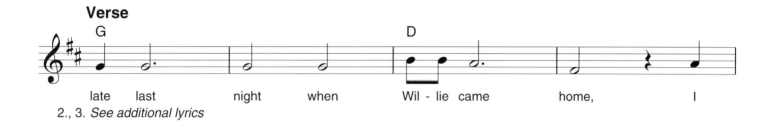

late   last   night   when   Wil - lie came   home,   I

2., 3. *See additional lyrics*

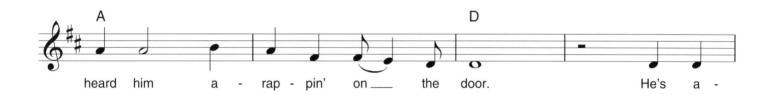

heard   him   a - rap - pin'   on ___   the   door.   He's   a -

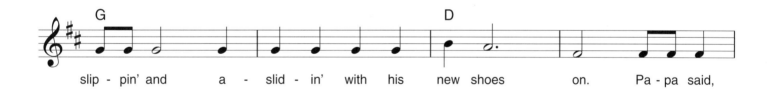

slip - pin' and   a - slid - in'   with   his   new   shoes   on.   Pa - pa said,

"Wil - lie don't   you   rap   no ___   more."

Additional Lyrics

2. Well, I wish I was over at my sweet Sally's house,
    A-sittin' in that big armchair.
    One arm around my old guitar,
    And the other one around my dear.

3. Now one old shirt is about all I've got,
    And a dollar is all that I crave.
    I brought nothing with me into this old world,
    Ain't gonna take nothing to my grave.

Standard Ukulele

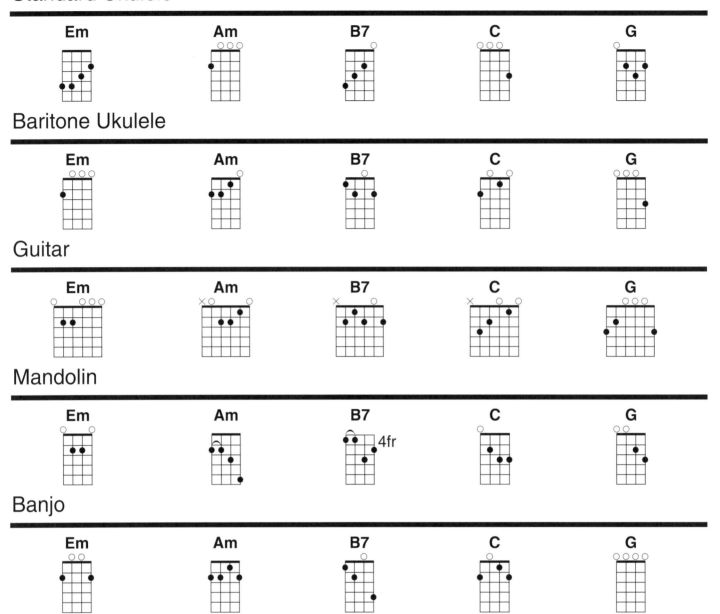

Baritone Ukulele

Guitar

Mandolin

Banjo

Wayfaring Stranger
Southern American Folk Hymn

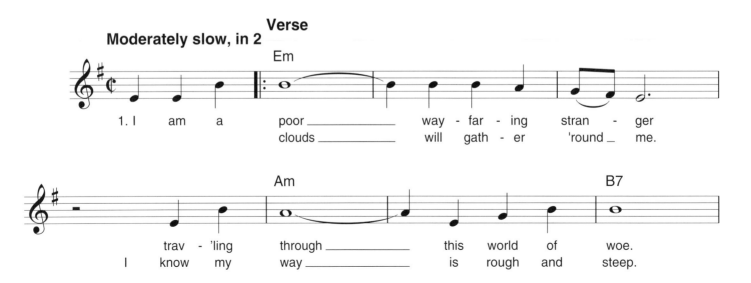

Verse
Moderately slow, in 2

Em

1. I am a poor _____ way - far - ing stran - ger
clouds _____ will gath - er 'round __ me.

Am   B7

trav - 'ling through _____ this world of woe.
I know my way _____ is rough and steep.

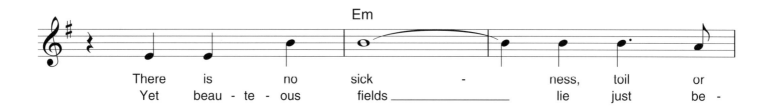

There is no sick - ness, toil or
Yet beau - te - ous fields _____ lie just be -

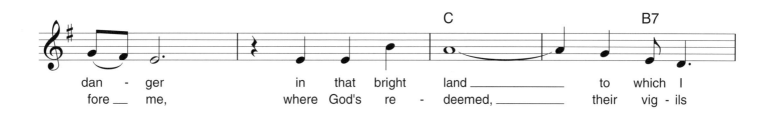

dan - ger in that bright land _____ to which I
fore __ me, where God's re - deemed, _____ their vig - ils

Chorus

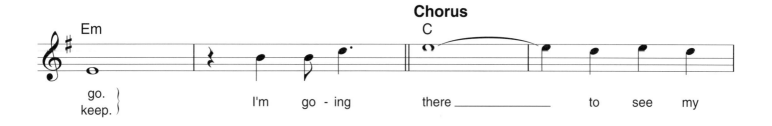

go.
keep. } I'm go - ing there _____ to see my

ma - ma. _____ She said she'd meet _____ me when I

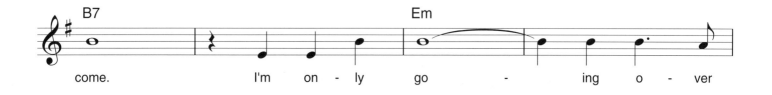

come. I'm on - ly go - ing o - ver

Jor - dan. I'm on - ly go - ing o - ver

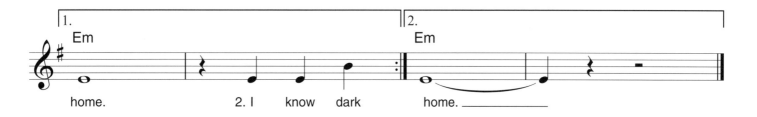

home. 2. I know dark home. _____

Standard Ukulele

Baritone Ukulele

Guitar

Mandolin

Banjo

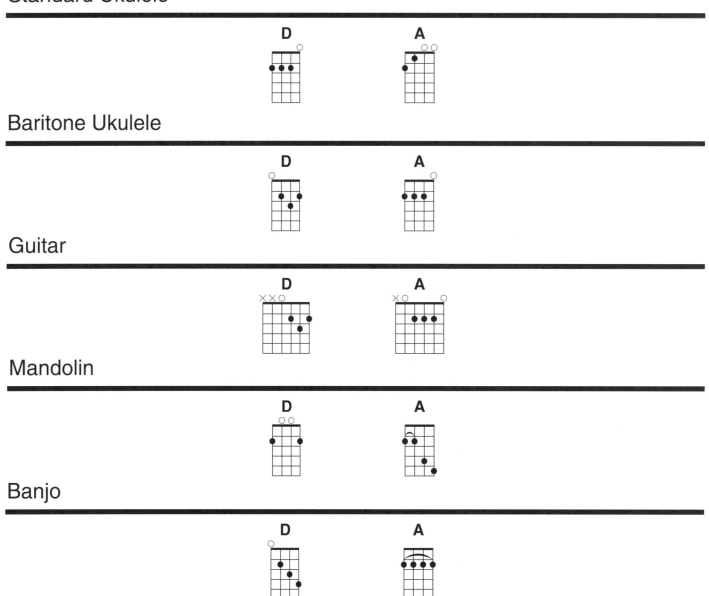

What Would You Give in Exchange for Your Soul

Words and Music by J.H. Carr and J.J. Berry

Medium Waltz

Verse

1. Broth - er a - far _____ from the Sa - vior to - day, _____

2., 3. *See additional lyrics*

_____ risk - ing your soul _____ for the

things that de - cay. _____ Oh, if to - day _____

_____ God should call __ you a - way, _____

what would you give _____ in ex -change for your soul? _____

Chorus

_____ What would you give (in ex - change), what would you

give (in ex - change), what would you give _____

_____ in ex -change for your soul? _____ Oh, if to -

day _____ God should call __ you a - way, _____

what would you give _____ in ex - change for your

1., 2.

soul? _____ 2. Mer - cy is soul? _____
3. More than the

3.

Additional Lyrics

2. Mercy is calling you; won't you give heed?
   Must the dear Savior still tenderly plead?
   Risk not your soul; it is precious indeed.
   What would you give in exchange for your soul?

3. More than the silver and gold of this earth,
   More than all jewels a spirit is worth.
   God the creator has given you birth.
   What would you give in exchange for your soul?

Standard Ukulele

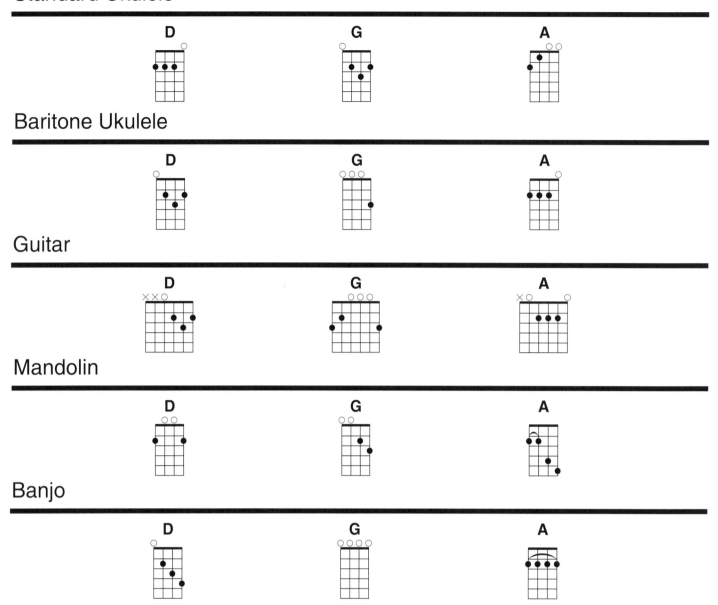

Baritone Ukulele

Guitar

Mandolin

Banjo

White Dove
Words and Music by Carter Stanley

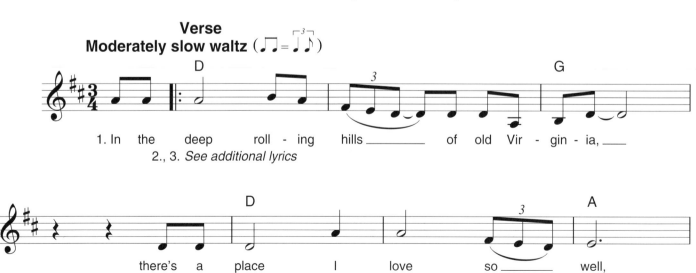

Verse
Moderately slow waltz

1. In the deep roll - ing hills _____ of old Vir - gin - ia, _____
2., 3. *See additional lyrics*

there's a place I love so _____ well,

where I spent man-y days _____ of my child-hood _

in a cab-in where we loved ___ to _____ dwell.

Chorus

White doves will mourn in sor-row; the

wil-lows will hang ___ their ___ heads. I'll live my

life in sor-row since Moth-er and

Dad-dy are ___ dead.

2. We were
3. As the

Additional Lyrics

2. We were all so happy there together
   In our peaceful little mountain home.
   But the Savior needs angels in heaven;
   Now they sing around that great white throne.

3. As the years roll by, I often wonder,
   Will we all be together some day?
   And each night as I wander through the graveyard,
   Darkness finds me where I kneel to pray.

Standard Ukulele

G 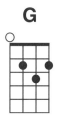 **G7** 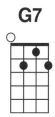 **C**  **D7**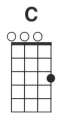

Baritone Ukulele

G 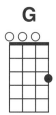 **G7** 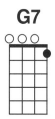 **C**  **D7**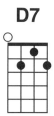

Guitar

G 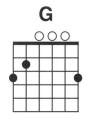 **G7** 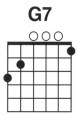 **C** 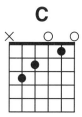 **D7**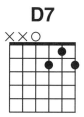

Mandolin

G  **G7** 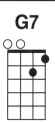 **C** 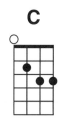 **D7**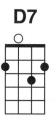

Banjo

G 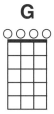 **G7** 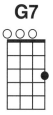 **C**  **D7**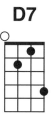

Will the Circle Be Unbroken

Words by Ada R. Habershon
Music by Charles H. Gabriel

Standard Ukulele

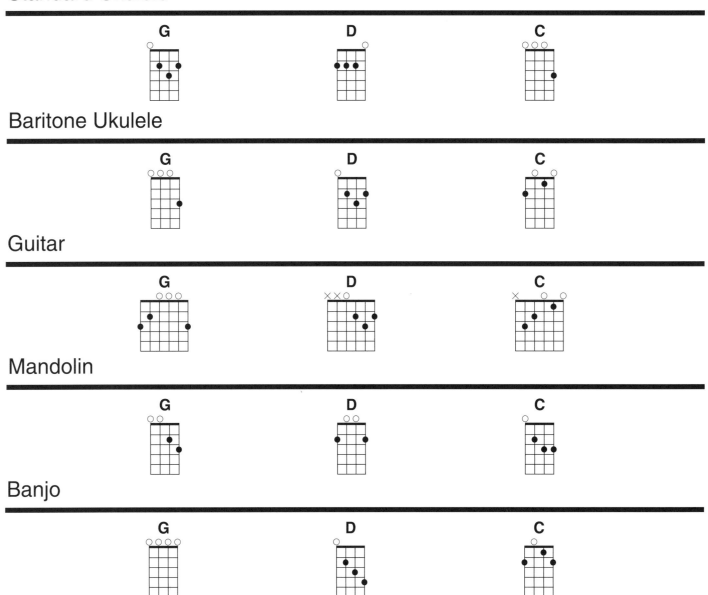

Baritone Ukulele

Guitar

Mandolin

Banjo

Will You Be Loving Another Man

Words and Music by Bill Monroe and Lester Flatt

Verse
Moderately, in 2

1. Now, will you love me, lit - tle dar - lin',
2., 3. *See additional lyrics*

when I'm in some oth - er land,

and you know I can't __ be with you, or will

you be lov - in' an - oth - er man? __ Will

Chorus

you be lov - ing an - oth - er man? Will

you be lov - ing an - oth - er man? When

I re - turn, will you __ be wait - ing, or will

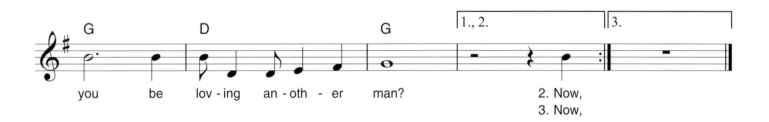

you be lov - ing an - oth - er man?

2. Now,
3. Now,

Additional Lyrics

2. Now, don't be crying on my shoulder
   And telling me that love is grand,
   And before I'm out of sight, dear,
   Then be loving another man.

3. Now, if I find this to be true, dear,
   I want you to please understand,
   When I return don't say you're sorry,
   Just keep on loving another man.

Standard Ukulele

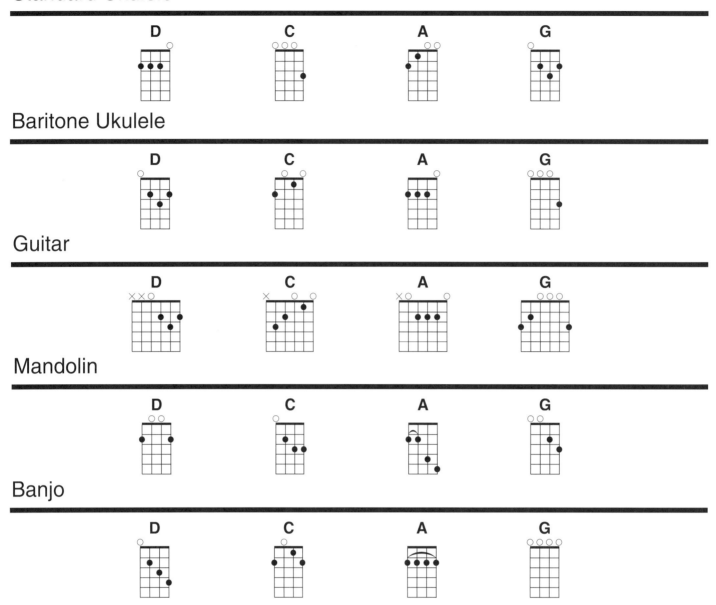

Baritone Ukulele

Guitar

Mandolin

Banjo

With Body and Soul

Words and Music by Virginia Stauffer

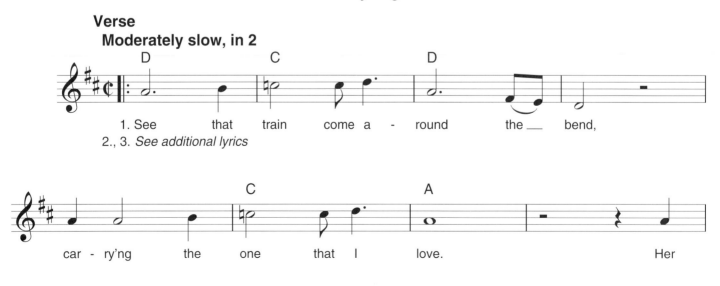

Verse
Moderately slow, in 2

1. See that train come a - round the __ bend,
2., 3. *See additional lyrics*

car - ry'ng the one that I love. Her

beau - ti - ful bod - y _____ is still here on earth, __

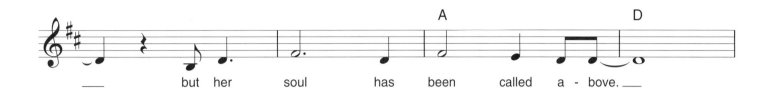

__ but her soul has been called a - bove. __

Chorus

Bod - y _____ and soul, _____ bod - y _____ and

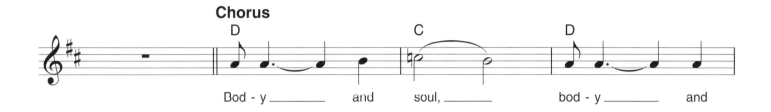

soul, that's how she loved me, with bod - y and

soul.   2. Her   That's how she
3. To -

loved me, with bod - y and soul.

Additional Lyrics

2. Her beautiful hair was the purest of gold;
   Her eyes were as blue as the sea.
   Her lips were the color of summer's red rose,
   And she promised she would always love me.

3. Tomorrow as the sun sinks low,
   The shadows will cover her face.
   Her last sun goes down as she's laid beneath the ground,
   And my teardrops are falling like rain.

Standard Ukulele

Baritone Ukulele

Guitar

Mandolin

Banjo

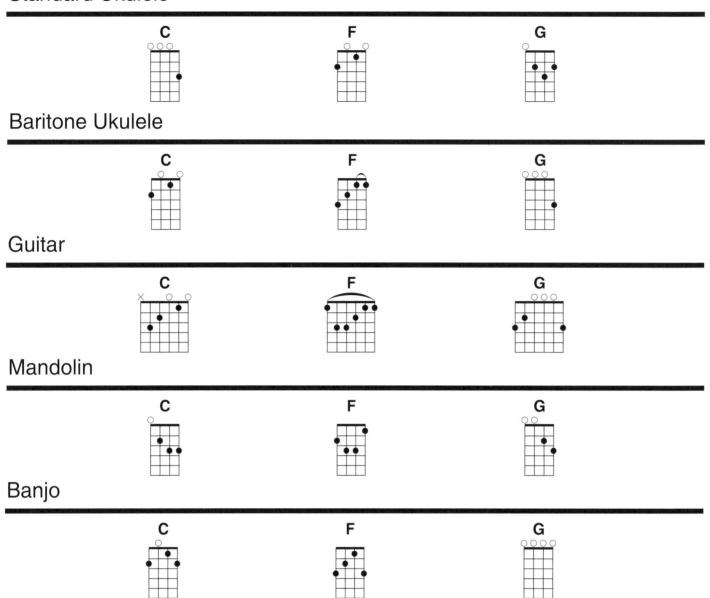

The Wreck of the Old '97
Words and Music by Henry Whitter, Charles Noell and Fred Lewey

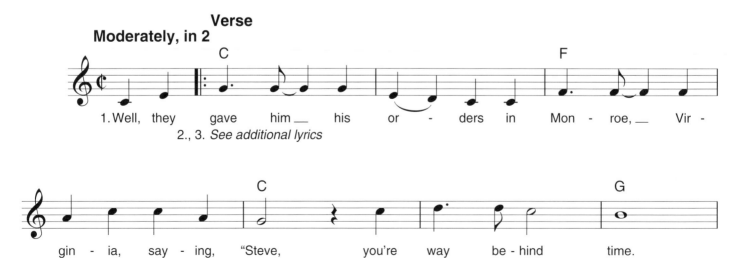

Verse

Moderately, in 2

1. Well, they gave him __ his or - ders in Mon - roe, __ Vir -

2., 3. *See additional lyrics*

gin - ia, say - ing, "Steve, you're way be - hind time.

Additional Lyrics

2. It's a mighty rough road from Lynchburg to Danville,
   And lined on a three-mile grade.
   It's on that grade that he lost his airbrakes;
   You see what a jump he made.
   They were going down grade making ninety miles an hour
   When his whistle broke into a scream.
   He was found in a wreck with his hand on the throttle,
   Was scalded to death by the steam.

3. Then a telegram came to Washington City,
   And this is how is read:
   The brave engineer that run old Ninety-Seven
   Is lying in old Danville dead.
   Now all you ladies need take warning
   From the time now and learn,
   Never speak harsh words to your true loving husband,
   He may leave you and never return.

Standard Ukulele

A	D	E7

Baritone Ukulele

A	D	E7
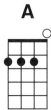		

Guitar

A	D	E7
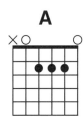	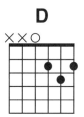	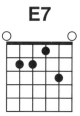

Mandolin

A	D	E7
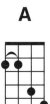	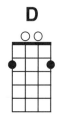	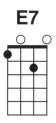

Banjo

A	D	E7
	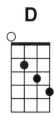	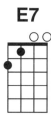

You Are My Sunshine

Words and Music by Jimmie Davis

Standard Ukulele

Baritone Ukulele

Guitar

Mandolin

Banjo

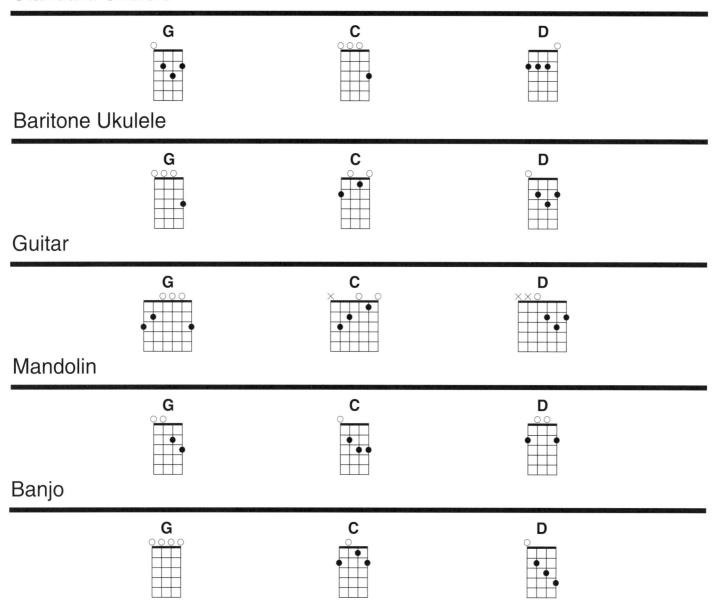

You Don't Know My Mind

Words and Music by Jimmie Skinner

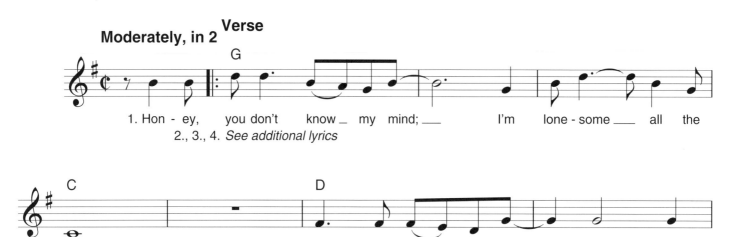

1. Hon - ey, you don't know __ my mind; __ I'm lone - some __ all the
2., 3., 4. *See additional lyrics*

time. Born to lose, __ a drift - er, that's

me. ___   You can trav - el   for ___ so   long, ___   then a

ram - bler's   heart ___ goes   wrong.   Ba - by, _____ you don't

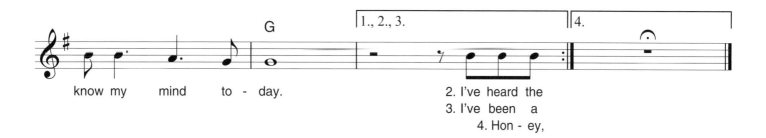

know my   mind   to - day.   2. I've heard the
                                       3. I've been   a
                                          4. Hon - ey,

Additional Lyrics

2. I've heard the music of the rail,
   Slept in every dirty jail.
   Life's too short for you to worry me.
   When I find that I can't win,
   I'll be checking out again.
   Baby, you don't know my mind today.

3. I've been a hobo and a tramp;
   My soul has done been stamped.
   Things I know I've learned the hard, hard way.
   When I find that I can't win,
   I'll be checking out again.
   Baby, you don't know my mind today.

4. Honey, you don't know my mind;
   I'm lonesome all the time.
   I've traveled fast on this hard road, you see.
   I'm not here to judge or plead,
   Just to give my poor heart ease.
   Baby, you don't know my mind today.

Tuning

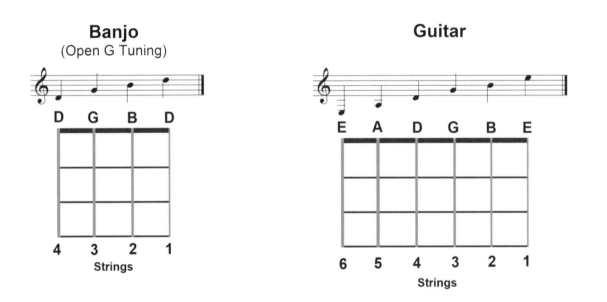

Standard Ukulele
(Soprano, Concert, Tenor)

G C E A

4 3 2 1
Strings

Baritone Ukulele

D G B E

4 3 2 1
Strings

Mandolin

G D A E

4 3 2 1
Strings

Banjo
(Open G Tuning)

D G B D

4 3 2 1
Strings

Guitar

E A D G B E

6 5 4 3 2 1
Strings

All banjo chord formations illustrated in this book are based on "Open G" tuning. If an alternate tuning is used the banjo player can read the chord letters for the songs and disregard the diagrams.